ROBERT L. WILSON holds the degree of Master of Arts (Oxon.) and diplomas in Education and English Studies. He taught for three years at Lord Williams's School, Thame, Oxfordshire, and for two years at Manchester Grammar School. He now works in the University of Oxford Department of Educational Studies, and has been examining at A-level for the Cambridge Examinations Syndicate for some years. He is the co-author of *Explore and Express*, a four-volume English course for secondary schools (Macmillan).

GCE O-Level Passbooks

GEOGRAPHY, R. Knowles, M.A.

MODERN MATHEMATICS, A. J. Sly, B.A.

HISTORY (*Social and Economic*, 1815–1939), M. C. James, B.A.

HISTORY (*Political and Constitutional*, 1815–1939), L. James, B.A., M.Litt.

FRENCH, G. Butler, B.A.

CHEMISTRY, C. W. Lapham, M.Sc.

BIOLOGY, R. Whitaker, B.Sc. and J. M. Kelly, B.Sc., M.I.Biol.

PHYSICS, B. P. Brindle, B.Sc.

ECONOMICS, J. E. Waszek, B.Sc. (Econ)

GCE O-Level Passbook

English Language

Robert L. Wilson, M.A.

Published by Intercontinental Book Productions
in conjunction with Seymour Press Ltd.

Distributed by Seymour Press Ltd.,
334 Brixton Road, London, SW9 7AG

Published 1976 by Intercontinental Book Productions, Berkshire House, Queen Street, Maidenhead, Berks., SL6 1NF in conjunction with Seymour Press Ltd.

1st edition, 10th impression 8.80.9
Copyright © 1976 Intercontinental Book Productions
Made and printed by C. Nicholls & Company Ltd
ISBN 0 85047 901 0

Contents

Chapter 1
Using this Book

Facts or skills?

English is rather different from many other school subjects in that it does not simply consist of a body of facts and information which must be studied, understood and thought about. There are, of course, facts which are relevant to the subject, such as the grammatical structure of our language, the way we use punctuation, the way we spell or set out different sorts of formal and informal writings, but knowledge of these matters does not, in itself, ensure that a student will be good at English, though such knowledge will obviously help. To be competent in the use of English, to be capable at this point in your career of passing the Ordinary-level GCE examination, means that you have mastered a range of skills rather than understood and absorbed a body of information.

We might compare the acquisition of the skills of English with learning to play a musical instrument. One may well know a great deal about musical theory and the structure of musical compositions yet be quite incapable of playing anything on an instrument. A skill, such as playing the piano, cannot be learnt without considerable and regular practice and this practice involves applying musical knowledge to the growing skill of performance. Progress is made when the performer's technical ability develops alongside his musical knowledge so that he is increasingly able to apply that knowledge to the pieces on which he is working. Neither theoretical knowledge alone nor technical skill alone will make a good musician: the two must develop together and support each other.

The same is true of learning the uses of language in reading and writing. You cannot avoid using these skills in everyday life and must already possess some basic competence or you would not be working for the English O-level examination, but real development of the capacity for reading and writing only takes place when the student is able to understand more and more of what these processes involve and is able to apply this understanding to the way he himself reads and writes.

This book has been designed to help you develop these skills. It contains many opportunities for practising them in a controlled way, so that you can apply to your own reading or writing the insights that the book is offering at that particular point. It must be emphasised that skills in the use of language simply cannot be acquired without practice. Just reading through this book should give you a greater appreciation of the ground to be covered and the sort of development that could take place in your use of language, but you will gain far more if you work through the exercises intelligently. This need not be drudgery: to be enlarging your capacity for understanding the writings of others and for expressing your thoughts and feelings in writing is an exhilarating experience. It is not at all a question of merely absorbing a few tips for passing an examination. What you are concerned with, in developing your capacity for communicating, is nothing less than the growth of your own personality, extending your sensitivity and awareness and your powers of thought and judgement. Try, then, to remember that you are not going through the motions of performing isolated exercises with only one end in view, which is the passing of a mere examination. You will indeed be acquiring skills which will enrich you for all your life.

Reading

Reading is a complex art in which we strive to gain something from what someone else is offering. When we read, we have to hold in check our own feelings and thoughts so that we may be open to those of the author. Good reading involves swiftly attuning ourselves to the author's patterns of thought and ways of perceiving the world so that we may gain the maximum possible effect from his writing. This is not easy but, as we grow in sensitivity to the immense possibilities of different and complex forms of literature, so it will become increasingly natural to adapt to the particular author's style and respond in the way he intended.

Let us consider for a moment the variety of demands that reading can make upon us. Here are two short passages, the first from a book on architecture, *The Cathedrals of England* by Harry Batsford and Charles Fry, and the second from D. H. Lawrence's novel, *The Rainbow*. Both passages focus on Lincoln cathedral.

A Of its many façades, the most ambitious is the screen wall of the west front in which ranks of lancet arcading, extending some 175 feet from north to south, are broken by three tremendous shadowed cavities rising over the Norman doors. The section of unrelieved wall in which these are set formed part of the fabric of the original church, and its panels of Romanesque figure-carving contrast curiously with the uncomfortably seated figures of fourteenth-century kings ranged over the central door. It is impossible here to analyse in any detail the complex evolution of this remarkable composition; but whatever its merits or demerits as a unit, it is unrelated to the design of the cathedral as a whole, and remains as was intended, purely a screen, above which the twin Perpendicular towers, with their lower ranges of Romanesque arcading, rise a trifle abruptly.

B They had passed through the gate, and the great west front was before them, with all its breadth and ornament.

"It is a false front," he said, looking at the golden stone and the twin towers, and loving them just the same. In a little ecstasy he found himself in the porch, on the brink of the unrevealed. He looked up to the lovely unfolding of the stone. He was to pass within to the perfect womb.

Then he pushed open the door, and the great, pillared gloom was before him, in which his soul shuddered and rose from her nest. His soul leapt, soared up into the great church. His body stood still, absorbed by the height.

The first passage primarily requires an intellectual attention, a concentration upon the information and thought which the authors present in relation to the west front of Lincoln cathedral, whilst passage B demands a response to the feelings of the man who is looking at the building and a sympathetic understanding of his intense experience. It is, of course, too simple just to say that A demands that we read thoughtfully and B that we read with feeling, since there are phrases in the first passage which imply a judgement of the building, based on a response of feeling, and we have, in passage B, to make the effort to understand, as well as to be moved by the man's reactions to the building. In the course of chapters 2, 3 and 4, we shall be closely examining the different types of attention and understanding that may be required of us from different sorts of writing. These chapters move generally from passages which demand a more emotional or sympathetic response, such as B above, towards the more detached, rational writing, of which A is an example. It would be best for you to take each of these chapters as a separate unit and work through the various exercises in comprehension that they contain. Suggested answers are provided at the end of the book but you will gain most benefit if you work through the exercises on your own before consulting them. Don't forget that you will only acquire the skills involved in understanding the writing of other people through practice: there is no short cut.

Writing

Chapters 5 to 10 are all designed to help you develop and refine your own writing skills. Again, a number of exercises have been included and within each chapter they gradually increase in difficulty. My main aim, in these chapters, has been to offer you ways of thinking constructively about your writing so that you can develop it knowing that writing is an infinitely varied and subtle form of communication. I have pointed to ways in which you can learn to control the content of your compositions and create the desired effect on your reader.

In these chapters, there is little about the rules of accurate writing, spelling and punctuation, nor is there any direct treatment of the examination itself. Short sections on these matters are therefore included towards the end of the book.

Finally, I am bound to say that a course book such as this is of little use if it is kept in isolation from the constant use of language — reading, writing and talking — that fills every part of your life. Apply the insights that you gain from the following chapters to all of your reading and writing. Every time you write a letter to a friend or an essay as part of the study of another subject, concentrate on being as precise in your use of English as possible and as imaginative as is appropriate to that particular piece of writing. Similarly, continue to read as widely as you can: newspapers, magazines, books of general interest, novels — I include a list of suitable novels at the end of this book. Above all, enjoy developing your skills in using language.

Chapter 2
Understanding People in Books

How characters are revealed

It is quite clear that almost every story, whether it be short or a full-length novel, is about people, people alone, in couples, in families or social groups. The absorbing interest in any novel is what the characters say, what they do, how they act towards one another, how they feel with this person or that person, how they feel when they are alone, how they react to new places or to old familiar haunts. Every novelist who is at all concerned about his characters and wishing to involve his reader in their personalities will be constantly developing situations in which his characters will reveal something of themselves. Just as knowing a person in real life is never a complete and final thing, so that even with people you know well you constantly find little unexpected details of their thoughts or feelings or notice that they react in a way you had not expected, so, in a book about people, every detail and every new situation may contribute to a richer understanding of the character.

The ways in which characters are revealed to us in a novel reflect the ways in which we come to know people in real life. On meeting someone for the first time, you would perhaps be most aware of his appearance and his manner towards you. As a friendship forms, you would be noticing the way your friend deals with other people, what his interests are, what makes him angry, happy, sad, and so on. You will learn about his background, his parents and a multitude of other matters which will all help to round out the picture of him which is developing in your mind. He will become more real, more of an individual to you and, as new facets of his personality become evident, you might find yourself changing your opinions of him or your feelings about him.

So it is in a novel. The author chooses details about the person's appearance, his physique, his clothes, his way of talking, his way of moving; he points perhaps to the way his face changes, what expression is revealed in the movement of his eyebrows, whether he appears surprised or calm or hurt or joyful at something that happens to him. If it is a good novel, then all these details will hold together in a unity and the character will seem, as we say, true to life. Also true to life will be the way in which we come to know a character in a good novel. The author will reveal to us just so much as he wants us to know about his characters at any one point in the narration. His skill in feeding us the right details in the right order may well give us the experience of getting to know his characters precisely as we get to know people in real life, our overall awareness of the person developing and becoming more three-dimensional as we read on. Furthermore, since a novel must of necessity be about events and events take place in time, the story of a novel must cover a length of time – which may be a mere couple of hours, or a day or two, or may span years. In the latter case particularly, we would expect the characters to change and develop, their attitudes and outlook on life to be modified by the experiences narrated so that they become perhaps more mature or humane people. As readers, we would want to be so attuned to these changes in the characters of the book that we would not miss any signs of their development or hints of growth. A good reader will not be interested simply in the story, the bald events of the novel: his feelings about the characters will be aroused and he will share in their experiences and sympathise with their feelings.

In a novel which contains well-conceived characters, there will be no irrelevant details about them. At every moment in the book, we will see the character doing things, thinking, feeling, speaking. These actions, thoughts, sensations or words will either be what we would have expected of him, or they will bring home to us aspects of his personality that we had not quite grasped, or, if it is a particularly significant moment in the novel, then how the character reacts may reveal a quite new aspect of his being and indicate that he has grown and changed as a person.

I stress the presence of these 'details' because normally, when reading a story or novel in a relaxed way, you would not stop to make a mental note that this detail or that is adding to your sense of the reality of a character. It would impede the flow of the story and the good reader would, in any case, be able to absorb most of these details quite naturally, without stopping to think about them in an artificial way. Bad readers, however, merely hasten forward, skimming over passages which seem to them to be too full of detail and description, wanting only to know what happens next. The habitual skimmer misses the richness of experience that a novel might offer him: he cannot sink himself into its world and identify with the characters, that is, he cannot understand them and feel as deeply as he might about them. A bad reader, a skimmer, is rather like someone who prefers to snatch a hasty sandwich rather than to enjoy a good meal.

The skill of appreciating people in books and of absorbing the details provided by the author in order that you should know all that he wants you to know about his characters can be developed by reading widely, with enjoyment and with sensitivity, stopping sometimes to listen attentively to the voice of the author. With experience, you will become aware that an author very often gives the reader signals or hints, that on occasion he writes between the lines in a subtle way that may not be obvious at first sight. It is very often the little, and apparently unimportant, details of description that convey the inner lives of the characters and may open them up to us. In the examination, there may well be questions on passages concerned with people, such questions being designed to test the candidate's skill in close and attentive reading and his capacity to appreciate the characters in the extract. If you are to answer these questions perceptively, you must develop the skill of identifying the telling details and then using all the evidence provided in the short passage in order to grasp a sense of the characters.

A moment of recognition

Let us begin by looking closely at a passage taken from about half-way through William Golding's novel, *Lord of the Flies*. This book is about a group of rather middle-class schoolboys who find themselves suddenly deposited on an uninhabited tropical island. They are of varying ages but the oldest is only about thirteen. They try to organise themselves so as to keep a sense of order and to look after the younger boys, and so they develop a system of holding assemblies or gatherings in which they can make decisions as a group. However, it becomes more and more difficult to hold the group together: there are many fears amongst the boys and rivalries between them. The following extract shows Ralph, one of the older boys and the one who has emerged as a leader, thinking about a coming assembly which will be vital if he is going to control the uncivilised and aggressive forces which are beginning to spread amongst the boys.

The tide was coming in and there was only a narrow strip of firm beach between the water and the white, stumbling stuff near the palm terrace. Ralph chose the firm strip as a path because he needed to think; and only here could he allow his

5   feet to move without having to watch them. Suddenly, pacing
by the water, he was overcome with astonishment. He found
himself understanding the wearisomeness of this life, where
every path was an improvisation and a considerable part of
one's waking life was spent watching one's feet. He stopped,
10 facing the strip; and remembering that first enthusiastic
exploration as though it were part of a brighter childhood, he
smiled jeeringly. He turned then and walked back towards
the platform with the sun in his face. The time had come for
the assembly and as he walked into the concealing splendours
15 of the sunlight he went carefully over the points of his speech.
There must be no mistake about this assembly, no chasing
imaginary ...

He lost himself in a maze of thoughts that were rendered
20 vague by his lack of words to express them. Frowning, he
tried again.

This meeting must not be fun, but business.

25 At that he walked faster, aware all at once of urgency and the
declining sun and a little wind created by his speed that
breathed about his face. This wind pressed his grey shirt
against his chest so that he noticed – in this new mood of
comprehension – how the folds were stiff like cardboard, and
30 unpleasant; noticed too how the frayed edges of his shorts
were making an uncomfortable, pink area on the front of his
thighs. With a convulsion of the mind, Ralph discovered dirt
and decay; understood how much he disliked perpetually
flicking the tangled hair out of his eyes, and at last, when the
35 sun was gone, rolling noisily to rest among dry leaves. At that,
he began to trot.

It is not easy to perceive at once exactly what state of mind Ralph
is experiencing. You might notice phrases like, 'the wearisomeness of this life' or details like Ralph's memory of the first
occasion when he and the other boys landed on this same 'narrow
strip of firm beach'. This memory causes him to smile 'jeeringly'.
Why?

Then he chooses the narrow strip of firm beach to walk along
because here he can walk unimpeded by all the tangled
undergrowth of a tropical island. But, in walking along it and

14

thinking, or rather trying to think, he is overcome with astonishment'. **Why does this happen? What sudden realisation comes to him?**

Why should choosing a firm and easy path to walk along set going a train of thought and association in Ralph's mind that leads to his regarding a happy memory of 'enthusiastic exploration' with a jeering smile? The answer lies in the statement: 'He found himself understanding the wearisomeness of this life, where every path was an improvisation and a considerable part of one's life was spent watching one's feet.' Ralph has, in fact, been forced to grow up, to grow up suddenly in a matter of days. He has had to abandon the attitude of childhood, where decisions are made by adults and the child, quite properly, can enjoy play and exhilaration because all around him is a stability and a known order created by grown-ups. As an adult, a man has to make his own way in life, find his own paths and generally avoid treading on other people's toes; he has to make his own decisions, get along with people and not 'put his foot in it'. Ralph's realisation that it is difficult to walk easily on the island because there are no paths means more than noticing physical obstacles: he is confronting all the difficulty of his life as a young boy prematurely forced into an adult role.

If you were asked the simple question, **'Explain, in the context of its use in the passage, the meaning of the phrase, "every path was an improvisation"'**, it would not be adequate to write, 'There were no paths on the island, so each time Ralph tried to go anywhere, he had to create a path for himself'. That would be quite true but it would not indicate that Golding has taken up a simple physical description and related it to something going on inside Ralph's mind. He suggests to us that Ralph's physical experience of trying to find his way across the island is matched by his mental experience of trying to find a way through all the decisions and uncertainties that face him as a leader of the group of boys.

Reading on through the passage, an obvious detail to notice is that as soon as Ralph perceives he can no longer act as a child but must take responsibility, he turns and walks back towards the platform because that is where the assembly will be held and where he must make an effective impact on the rest of the boys. His turning back is his facing of responsibility. Yet he finds this very difficult: his thoughts tend to get out of hand and the phrase 'the concealing splendours of the sunlight', as well as describing the difficulty of seeing clearly when the sun is in his eyes, low in the sky, also suggests that fantasy and the chasing of imaginary possibilities is a way to avoid facing up to what he has got to do. Fantasy and vagueness cast an attractive glow over life and make it difficult to see clearly. Ralph has to make a further effort of thought and, having told himself that this meeting must be serious and not fun, he walks faster and eventually trots back to the assembly place. His physical movements again suggest the state of his mind with its growing sense of urgency. Try now to answer the question, **'How do Ralph's physical actions reflect his state of mind throughout this extract?'**

If you have noticed carefully the details of his movements, the way he chooses the firm strip and begins to walk along it, his stopping when he realises how far he is from the happy carefree innocence of childhood, his turning back as he accepts responsibility for the conduct of the assembly and his assuming a faster pace as the sense of urgency mounts in him, with his beginning to trot as a further perception comes to him at the end of this extract, you will not find that question hard to deal with. To answer it well, however, you would need to have both visualised the situation of Ralph on the beach and also to have sympathetically shared in his state of mind and to do that well you must take note of all the details, however minor they may at first appear.

Similarly, with regard to the final paragraph, one might ask the question, **'Explain the full meaning, in the context of this passage, of the phrase, "this new mood of comprehension" (lines 28–9)'.**

It does not carry us very far to provide a dictionary definition, such as, 'This state of mind in which a new understanding of life was reached'. It is necessary to look at what is being described in that paragraph, and how it carries us further into understanding what is happening inside Ralph. He suddenly becomes far more aware than he had been before of what his clothes and body have become since he has been on the island. His senses are sharpened: he notices the declining sun and the breeze on his face caused by his quickened pace and he sees dirt on his clothes and his body and realises, for the first time, how much he dislikes the condition in which he is forced to live. One imagines that before this moment he might have been vaguely aware of discomfort, sensed somehow that things were not all that they ought to be. Now, because he has

16

recognised the challenge and difficulties facing him and made a stern effort to confront them, he is able to grasp clearly what before would have been only a sequence of vague sensations. That sudden recognition of the nature of his life on the island came, as Golding says, as 'a convulsion of the mind': it is like a revelation and his view of life generally will be permanently changed from this moment. His circumstances have forced him to discover what he really likes, he has made an important step towards finding his own tastes, his own likings and dislikes, and he is, therefore, that much more of an individual, a mature human being, able to discriminate and to make decisions about what he wants to do and what he is going to do.

The following couple of questions will help you to crystallise your thoughts about this passage. Make the effort to put into words your own perceptions. Like Ralph, try to avoid getting lost in a maze of thoughts rendered vague by lack of words to express them. You will, of course, need to read the passage again and to keep referring back to it. Suggested answers may be found on page 206.

1. Gather evidence from the passage to indicate as fully as you can what life is like for the boys on the island.

2. How does Ralph's state of mind change during his walk along the beach? There are at least four distinguishable moments of development.

A way of life

Whereas the previous passage presented us with a moment in a person's life, the passage that follows gives us a more general picture of an individual, what he looks like, what he habitually does, how he spends his life, what his surroundings are like and what he usually thinks and feels. It is more of a general character study than the exploration of a particular and significant event in a man's life. Yet the material is not presented in paragraphs each concerned with a separate aspect of all this: details of his physical appearance are interwoven with description of his surroundings, so that the man emerges before us in a real-life context. Similarly, his habitual thoughts and feelings are not presented all at once but arise bit by bit as we watch him perform a characteristic sequence of actions.

This passage is a simple routine moment in the life of a middle-aged man but it is written in such a way that by the time we reach the end of this extract, we know a lot about his circumstances and pattern of life, we understand his usual state of mind and we have some sympathy and feeling for him. We have the sense of encountering this character much as we might meet someone in real life, though, of course, the author is able to take us into the man's inner world. When you come to think about the character after reading the passage and attempt to summarise and put into words what you consider to be the important aspects of his life and personality, you will have to gather together evidence from different parts of the passage. It is the opening to a short story, by Allan Sillitoe, called 'Uncle Ernest', and the fact that it is a short story is perhaps the main reason for the author's so swiftly introducing us into the recesses of Uncle Ernest's mind and feelings.

A middle-aged man wearing a dirty raincoat, who badly needed a shave and looked as though he hadn't washed for a month, came out of a public lavatory with a cloth bag of tools folded beneath his arm. Standing for a moment on the edge of
5 the pavement to adjust his cap – the cleanest thing about him – he looked casually to left and right and, when the flow of traffic had eased off, crossed the road. His name and trade were always spoken in one breath, even when the nature of his trade was not in question: Ernest Brown the upholsterer.
10 Every night before returning to his lodgings he left the bag of tools for safety with a man who looked after the public lavatory near the town centre, for he felt there was a risk of them being lost or stolen should he take them back to his room, and if such a thing were to happen his living would be
15 gone.

Chimes to the value of half past ten boomed from the Council-house clock. Over the theatre patches of blue sky held hard-won positions against autumnal clouds, and a
20 treacherous wind lashed out its gusts, sending paper and cigarette packets cartwheeling along unswept gutters. Empty-bellied Ernest was ready for his breakfast, so walked through a café doorway, instinctively lowering his head as he did so, though the beams were a foot above his height.
25
The long spacious eating-place was almost full. Ernest usually arrived for his breakfast at nine o'clock, but having been paid ten pounds for re-covering a three-piece in a public house the

day before, he had stationed himself in the Saloon Bar for the
30 rest of the evening to drink jar after jar of beer, in a slow,
prolonged and concentrated way that lonely men have. As a
result it had been difficult to drag himself from drugged and
blissful sleep this morning. His face was pale and his eyes an
unhealthy yellow: when he spoke only a few solitary teeth
35 showed behind his lips.

Having passed through the half dozen noisy people standing
about he found himself at the counter, a scarred and chipped
haven for hands, like a littered invasion beach extending
40 between two headlands of tea urns. The big fleshy brunette
was busy, so he hastily scanned the list written out in large
white letters on the wall behind. He made a timid gesture
with his hand. "A cup of tea, please."

45 The brunette turned on him. Tea swilled from a huge brown
spout — into a cup that had a crack emerging like a hair above
the layer of milk — and a spoon clinked after it into the steam.
"Anything else?"

50 He spoke up hesitantly. "Tomatoes on toast as well." Picking
up the plate pushed over to him he moved slowly backwards
out of the crowd, then turned and walked towards a vacant
corner table.

55 A steamy appetising smell rose from the plate: he took up the
knife and fork and, with the sharp clean action of a craftsman,
cut off a corner of the toast and tomato and raised it slowly to
his mouth, eating with relish and hardly noticing people
sitting roundabout. Each wielding of his knife and fork, each
60 geometrical cut of the slice of toast, each curve and twist of his
lips joined in a complex and regular motion that gave him
great satisfaction. He ate slowly, quietly and contentedly,
aware only of himself and his body being warmed and made
tolerable once more by food. The leisurely movement of
65 spoon and cup and saucer made up the familiar noise of late
breakfast in a crowded café, sounded like music flowing here
and there in variations of rhythm.

For years he had eaten alone, but was not yet accustomed to
70 loneliness. He could not get used to it, had only adapted
himself to it temporarily in the hope that one day its spell
would break. Ernest remembered little of his past, and life

moved under him so that he hardly noticed its progress.
There was no strong memory to entice him to what had gone
75 by, except that of dead and dying men straggling barbed-wire
between the trenches in the first world war. Two sentences
had dominated his lips during the years that followed: "I
should not be here in England. I should be dead with the rest
of them in France." Time bereft him of these sentences, till
80 only a dull wordless image remained.

Before proceeding further, I suggest you write answers to the
following questions. You will need to read the passage carefully
again and keep referring back to it. When you have finished
writing, read the comments printed below the questions and see if
you can improve your answers before you compare them with the
suggested answers on page 206.

1. What evidence is there in this passage to suggest that Ernest
   Brown is a cautious, careful man?

2. Sillitoe says at a couple of points in the extract that Ernest is a
   lonely man. Is there anything that suggests to you that he is not
   entirely unhappy in his loneliness?

3. Explain in your own words exactly why Ernest has adopted his
   way of living in isolation from other people.

4. Comment on the meaning and effectiveness of the following
   phrases:
   'like a littered invasion beach extending between two headlands
   of tea urns' (lines 39–40);
   'like music flowing here and there in variations of rhythm'
   (lines 66–7);
   'life moved under him so that he hardly noticed its progress'
   (lines 72–3); 'till only a dull wordless image remained' (lines
   79–80).

Ernest Brown is first presented to us in terms of his trade and not
essentially as a person in his own right. Other people regard him as
'the upholsterer' rather than see him as an individual who happens
to do a certain job. He apparently defines himself in the same way
and goes to considerable length to preserve his livelihood by
leaving his tools for safety with a lavatory attendant rather than
suffer any anxiety on their account by taking them home. It is as if
he can take no responsibility for himself as a private individual: he

enjoys the food he buys, he has enjoyed his 'drugged and blissful sleep' and presumably relished his previous evening's drinking, but he takes no further care over himself. He is unshaven and dirty and he looks unwell and unwholesome with his 'few solitary teeth' and pallid face.

It is clear that Ernest does not live in any vital sense: it is as if he wishes to hide any feelings or any forcefulness that might yet lurk in his personality. So all his actions are slow and deliberate and suggest caution: the way he crosses the road, the careful and unnecessary lowering of his head as he enters the café doorway, his drinking of his beer the previous evening 'in a slow, prolonged and concentrated way'. Most of his actions are ritualised and routined; it is clearly a relief to him when he is settled at his isolated corner table and can concentrate only on the simple activity of eating. He then becomes so absorbed in his own movements that he is 'aware only of himself', quite cut off from all the bustle around him.

Ernest encounters only one person in the course of this passage: the brunette who is serving at the counter. His manner before her is timid and diffident. It is as if he feels himself to be without any right to ask for his cup of tea and tomatoes on toast. He accepts whatever he is given and makes as few demands on life as it is conceivable for a man to make. He has reduced his life to the barest of essentials, just work, sleeping, drinking and eating.

Why has this happened? What has made Ernest Brown into such a withdrawn, neurotic casualty of life? It is in the final paragraph that Sillitoe reveals how his experience as a survivor of the trench warfare of the First World War has so affected him. His experience there had been so traumatic and violent as to obliterate all the significance that the rest of life might have held for him. His memory of the 'dead and dying men straggling barbed-wire' is the only strong link that he has with his past. He has nothing else within him that he can build on and no feelings for ordinary human relationships. He believed himself to be a sort of ghost who should have died in France and to be consequently unworthy of any significant relationship with another person.

Three of the phrases to which I have drawn your attention in question 4 above describe Ernest's inner world, his sense of what life is like around and within him. They show him to be detached from any precise or sharp awareness of his surroundings or his own thoughts: all the little individual sounds of the café seem to him to be merged together in music, just as the sentences that had expressed what he really thought about his survival from the war had merged with the one visual memory of the trenches. So life passed him by, like some subterranean stream with which he had nothing to do. Only the description of the counter, 'like a littered invasion beach', seems to refer to the fighting element in ordinary life from which Ernest has withdrawn. We noticed how mild he is with the woman who serves the tea, although she is quite abrupt and aggressive in manner towards him. Reading through the passage, that reference to an invasion beach prepares us for the later explanation of his loneliness, his need to bury any memory of fighting.

Having pondered on my commentary, you should now return to your written answers and attempt to improve them by applying any further insights into the passage that you may have gained. You will have realised that I have not offered you direct answers to the questions. The commentary is intended rather to stimulate more general thought about the passage and appreciation of its contents. You should have more insights now from which to choose material appropriate to your answers: in answering this sort of comprehension question, it is always important to choose your references carefully. Your answers must be as precise and relevant as possible and there is no point in including any material which does not directly answer the question.

Characters in relationship with each other

Both the passages we have so far looked at in this chapter have dealt with individuals alone and from them we have been able to draw a considerable amount of information and insight into their personalities and present circumstances. Both passages are likely to have left you with a sense of expectation, curiosity about what is going to happen next to these people. Is Ralph going to be able to deal adequately with the assembly of boys? Will he be able to maintain his new-found sense of responsibility when he is actually faced with awkwardness and misunderstanding amongst them? Similarly, one might ask whether Uncle Ernest will always be alone. Will his day involve him in coming into contact with other people? How will they react to him and he to them? One could go on elaborating such speculation. The point here is that when we start to think about people, it is very difficult to think of them in isolation from others. Rarely does a work of fiction confine itself to a single character's thoughts and feelings just as few people are concerned about themselves in total isolation from others. Indeed, it is precisely because of Ernest's isolation that we are likely to find him a disturbing or at least a sad character. We pass on, therefore, to consider some passages in which people are found in various relationships with each other.

A work situation

Alexander Solzhenitsyn's novel, *One Day in the Life of Ivan Denisovich*, is a stark description of life in a Siberian labour camp. Its inmates are forced to live in the most severe conditions and they must fight for every morsel of food or minor comfort that might come their way. It is in the depths of winter but the 'zeks' or prisoners have each day to march some distance to work at building a new power-station. Yet, in spite of the terrible circumstances, these men, as we shall see from the following passage, are able to gain satisfaction from their work and this produces rapport and understanding between them.

There are a number of characters in this extract but we are primarily concerned with Ivan Denisovich Shukhov, simply referred to as Shukhov by his fellow prisoners. The whole book focuses on his actions and preoccupations during an average day in the labour camp. As you read through, notice the relationship he has with his team leader, Tiurin, and his work-mate, Senka. When the extract begins, night has started to fall and the men have to rush to finish their work before they march back to their camp. Tools have to be returned to the tool-store and the men mustered and lined up without any waste of time. They would want to work until the last moment because food rations for each team depend on the amount of work the team is able to complete.

Tiurin himself realised that he'd cut things too fine. The man in charge of the tool-store must be showering a dozen oaths on him.

5 "Eh," he shouted, "don't spare the shit! Carriers! Go and scrape the big box and out with what's left into that hole there and scatter some snow on it to keep it hidden. You, Pavlo, take a couple of men, collect the tools and hand them in. I'll send Gopchick after you with the three trowels. We'll use up
10 the last two loads of mortar before we knock off."

Everyone dashed to his job. They took Shukhov's hammer from him and wound up his string. The mortar-carriers and the block-lifters hurried down into the mortar-shop. They'd nothing more to do up there. Three masons remained on top, Kilgas, Senka, and Shukhov. Tiurin walked about to see how much wall they'd built. He was pleased. "Not bad, eh? In half a day. Without any fucking hoist."

Shukhov noticed there was a little mortar left in Kilgas's hod. He didn't want to waste it, but was worried that the team-leader might be reprimanded if the trowels were handed in late.

"Listen, lads," he said, "give your trowels to Gopchick. Mine's not on the list. There's no need to hand it in. I'll keep going."

Tiurin said with a laugh:

"How can we ever let you out? We just can't spare you."

Shukhov laughed too and went on working.

Kilgas took the trowels. Senka went on handing blocks to Shukhov. They poured Kilgas's mortar into Shukhov's hod.

Gopchick ran across to the tool-store, to overtake Pavlo. The rest were as anxious to be in time, and hurried over to the gates, without Tiurin. A team-leader is a power, but the escort is a greater power still. They list late-comers, and that means the cells for you.

There was a terrible crowd near the gates now. Everyone had collected there. It looked as if the escort had come out and started counting.

(They counted the prisoners twice on the way out: once before they unbolted the gates, to make sure they were safe in opening them, and again when the gates had been opened and the prisoners were passing through. And if they thought they'd miscounted, they recounted outside the gates.)

"To hell with the mortar," said Tiurin, with a gesture of impatience. "Sling it over the wall."

55 "Don't wait, leader. Go ahead, you're needed there."
(Shukhov usually addressed Tiurin, more respectfully, as
Andrei Prokofievich but now, after working like that, he felt
equal to the team-leader. He didn't put it to himself "Look,
I'm your equal", he just knew it.) And as Tiurin strode down
60 the ramp he called after him, jokingly: "Why do these rats
make the work-day so short? We're just getting into our
stride when they call it off."

Shukhov was left alone now with Senka. You couldn't say
65 much to him. Besides, you didn't have to tell him things: he
was the wisest of them all, he understood without need of
words.

Slap on the mortar. Down with the blocks. Press it home. See
70 it's straight. Mortar, Block. Mortar. Block . . .

Wasn't it enough that Tiurin had told them himself not to
bother about the mortar? Just throw it over the wall and
bugger off. But Shukhov wasn't made that way; eight
75 years in a camp couldn't change his nature. He worried
about anything he could make use of, about every scrap of
work he could do — nothing must be wasted without good
reason.

80 Mortar. Block. Mortar. Block . . .

"Finish, fuck you," shouted Senka. "Let's hop it."
He picked up a barrow and ran down the ramp.

85 But Shukhov — and if the guards had put the dogs on him it
would have made no difference — ran to the back and looked
about. Not bad. Then he ran and gave the wall a good look
over, to the left, to the right. His eye was as accurate as a spirit
level. Straight and even. His hands were as young as ever. He
90 dashed down the ramp.

Senka was already out of the mortar-shop and running down
the slope.

95 "Come on, come on," he shouted over his shoulder.

"Run on. I'll catch up," Shukhov gestured.

But he went into the mortar-shop. He couldn't simply throw
his trowel down. He might not be there the next day. They
100 might send the team off to the 'Socialist Way of Life'
settlement. It could be six months before he returned to the
power-station. But did that mean he was to throw down his
trowel? If he'd pinched it he had to hang on to it.

105 Both the stoves had been doused. It was dark, frightening.
Frightening not because it was dark but because everyone had
left, because he alone might be missing at the count by the
gates, and the guards would beat him.

110 Yet his eyes darted here, darted there, and, spotting a big
stone in the corner, he pulled it aside, slipped his trowel under
it, and hid it. So that's that.

Now to catch up with Senka. Senka had stopped after running
115 a hundred paces or so. Senka would never leave anyone in a
jam. Answer for it? Then together.

They ran level, the tall and the short. Senka was a head taller
than Shukhov, and a big head it was too.
120
There are loafers who race one another of their own free will
round a stadium. Those devils should be running after a full
day's work, with aching back and wet mittens and worn-out
valenki—and in the cold too.
125
They panted like mad dogs. All you could hear was their
hoarse breathing.

Write brief answers to the following questions. They are quite
simple, designed to help you become aware of some of the details
of the situation and to closely appreciate the reactions of the men. It
would be best to complete all the questions set on this passage and
to read the few paragraphs of commentary which follow the
questions before proceeding to check them against the suggested
answers on page 207.

1. For what reason do the men rush to carry out the instructions
given by Tiurin in lines 5–10?

2. How is it possible for Shukhov to continue working when all the tools have been returned to the tool-store?

3. What conflict does Shukhov experience in himself in lines 20–2 and how does he resolve it?

4. Why does Tiurin joke with Shukhov in line 30?

5. What prompts Tiurin's gesture of impatience in lines 53–4?

6. Explain the joke in lines 60–2. How would you describe Shukhov's mood during this interchange with Tiurin (lines 53–62)?

7. What two actions does Shukhov perform after Senka has left him on the building site? What motivates him to perform them?

8. What different sources of fear does Solzhenitsyn distinguish between in lines 105–8?

9. Why does the author contrast Senka and Shukhov with competitive athletes in lines 121–4?

The following questions are more difficult and require reference to a number of minor incidents in the passage and rather longer answers. You should read my commentary and attempt to improve your answers before checking them.

10. Use all the evidence provided in this passage to describe Shukhov's relationship with Tiurin. In your answer indicate how these particular circumstances make the relationship different from what it normally is.

11. Twice Shukhov has thoughts about Senka in the course of this incident. What are his feelings towards Senka? What sort of man does he appear to Shukhov to be?

12. How is Shukhov's concern for his work shown in this passage? There are at least three aspects of his concern shown here.

13. (a) What qualities of character have been fostered in Shukhov and Senka as a result of being in the labour camp?

(b) Pick out one quality of character in each of these men which has not been changed by being in the camp.

This passage has described one of the high points in Ivan Denisovich Shukhov's 'day'. He is a craftsman who takes pride in his work and, as a result, he experiences exhilaration in the vigorous activity into which he puts all his energy. His concern to make use of all the mortar, his care over his own trowel and his pleasure in looking over the completed piece of wall bear witness to his skill and to his conscientiousness. His enjoyment of his work, despite the demoralising effects of the labour camp with all its constrictions – and we are reminded of these in the description of the way the prisoners are counted and to the frequent references to the men's fears of punishment for any minor offence – is remarkably uplifting. It is as if the author is showing us that even in the worst circumstances imaginable, the human spirit is capable of triumphing and taking positive action.

The relationships that emerge here are dependent on this work-spirit. Shukhov, in his exhilaration, takes the initiative in suggesting to Tiurin that the tools be returned whilst he continues to work. That provokes the team-leader's praise, 'How can we ever let you out?', and this praise, in turn, modifies Shukhov's usual deference to Tiurin so that he dispenses with his formal name and talks to him as an equal. There is a spirit of good-fellowship between them and a bonhomie that issues in Shukhov's laughing complaint at the shortness of the working-day. Such a comment is almost inconceivable when you consider the drudgery and hardship of their lives.

Similarly, Shukhov and Senka are drawn together through their work. Senka continues to act as Shukhov's mate although the team-leader has told them to stop and throw the rest of the mortar away and, a little later on, he expresses his comradeship by waiting for Shukhov although it is vital that neither of them lose a second in getting to the gates. Shukhov relishes his mate's consideration: 'Senka would never leave anyone in a jam. Answer for it?'

You will, I expect, have noticed how little Solzhenitsyn is attempting to elaborate his descriptions of the scene and the state of things. Nearly everything is described briefly and factually. He is concerned only to convey exactly how life is experienced by the prisoners and to let this stark reality speak for itself. Only towards the end of the passage does he use a comparison to convey his feelings about the injustice of camp life when he contrasts the weary and frightened running of the two men to that of free athletes in a stadium. Exhaustion and deprivation are thus brought into contrast with healthy, life-giving exercise. His use of the word 'loafers' suggests his bitterness. Otherwise, his description is as stark and unadorned as the way of life he is describing.

Finally, there is an important point to be drawn from our consideration of this passage. It is a point, moreover, which you should remember whenever you are seeking to appreciate and understand a piece of writing which concerns itself with people together in a situation of any sort. This is that relationships are themselves modified and expressed through the circumstances in which the people are placed. People in books, as in life, are not finished products who act as automatons once their characters have been established. They are constantly changing and developing and their relationships likewise change and develop according to the circumstances. Shukhov would not have been as aware of his fellows nor have had the same feelings about them, if they had not been drawn into good-fellowship through their working together. In real life, your feelings for another person must inevitably be constantly shifting and changing – within a certain range, of course – as you go through different experiences together. So it is in a novel. Characters are not static if the novel is any good and you need, in looking at a passage about people, to be aware of what circumstances are influencing them and how the characters are influencing each other.

Love

In contrast to *One Day in the Life of Ivan Denisovich*, D. H. Lawrence's novel, *Sons and Lovers*, is very richly described and the reader's attention is less directed towards relationships that result from the circumstances of a group of people being forcibly brought together. Lawrence's concern is to explore the depths of his characters' personalities and to show how their deepest impulses are involved in the relationships they form. Inevitably, since he is dealing with instinctive forces, one of his main concerns is the sexual impulse and the book traces the development of a young man, Paul Morel, towards adulthood. His first relationship with a girl occurs when he visits a family who live in the country a few miles from his home. To begin with, he gravitates towards the mother and one of the sons, but Miriam, the only daughter in the family, is attracted to Paul and seeks to draw him into intimacy with her. She encourages his interest in painting and art and, in the following extract, wants him to share her intense pleasure in 'a certain wild-rose bush she had discovered'.

They came out upon the high road to Alfreton, which ran white between the darkening fields. There Paul hesitated. It was two miles home for him, one mile forward for Miriam. They both looked up the road that ran in shadow right under
5 the glow of the north-west sky. On the crest of the hill, Selby, with its stark houses and the up-pricked headstocks of the pit, stood in black silhouette small against the sky.

He looked at his watch.

10

"Nine o'clock!" he said.

The pair stood, loth to part, hugging their books.

15 "The wood is so lovely now," she said. "I wanted you to see it."

He followed her slowly across the road to the white gate.

20 "They grumble so if I'm late," he said.

"But you're not doing anything wrong," she answered impatiently.

25 He followed her across the nibbled pasture in the dusk. There was a coolness in the wood, a scent of leaves, of honey-suckle, and a twilight. The two walked in silence. Night came wonderfully there, among the throng of dark-trunks. He looked round expectant.

30

She wanted to show him a certain wild-rose bush she had discovered. She knew it was wonderful. And yet, till he had seen it, she felt it had not come into her soul. Only he could make it her own, immortal. She was dissatisfied.

35

Dew was already on the paths. In the old-oak wood a mist was rising, and he hesitated, wondering whether one whiteness were a strand of fog or only campion-flowers pallid in a cloud.

40 By the time they came to the pine-trees Miriam was getting
    very eager and very intense. Her bush might be gone. She
    might not be able to find it; and she wanted it so much.
    Almost passionately she wanted to be with him when he
    stood before the flowers. They were going to have a
45 communion together – something that thrilled her, some-
    thing holy. He was walking beside her in silence. They were
    very near to each other. She trembled, and he listened,
    vaguely anxious.

50 Coming to the edge of the wood, they saw the sky in front,
    like mother-of-pearl, and the earth growing dark. Some-
    where on the outermost branches of the pine-wood the
    honeysuckle was streaming scent.

55 "Where?" he asked.

    "Down the middle path," she murmured, quivering.

    When they turned the corner of the path she stood still. In the
60 wide walk between the pines, gazing rather frightened, she
    could distinguish nothing for some moments; the greying
    light robbed things of their colour. Then she saw her bush.

    "Ah!" she cried, hastening forward.
65
    It was very still. The tree was tall and straggling. It had
    thrown its briers over a hawthorn-bush, and its long
    streamers trailed thick right down to the grass, splashing the
    darkness everywhere with great split stars, pure white. In
70 bosses of ivory and in large splashed stars the roses gleamed
    on the darkness of foliage and stems and grass. Paul and
    Miriam stood close together, silent, and watched. Point after
    point the steady roses shone out of them, seeming to kindle
    something in their souls. The dusk came like smoke around,
75 and still did not put out the roses.

    Paul looked into Miriam's eyes. She was pale and expectant
    with wonder, her lips were parted, and her dark eyes lay open
    to him. His look seemed to travel down into her. Her soul
80 quivered. It was the communion she wanted. He turned
    aside, as if pained. He turned to the bush.

    "They seems as if they walk like butterflies, and shake
    themselves," he said.

85   She looked at her roses. They were white, some incurved and holy, others expanded in an ecstasy. The tree was dark as a shadow. She lifted her hand impulsively to the flowers; she bent forward and touched them in worship.

90   "Let us go," he said.

There was a cool scent of ivory roses — a white, virgin scent. Something made him feel anxious and imprisoned. The two walked in silence.
95
"Till Sunday," he said quietly, and left her; and she walked home slowly, feeling her soul satisfied with the holiness of the night. He stumbled down the path. And as soon as he was out of the wood, in the free open meadow, where he could
100   breathe, he started to run as fast as he could. It was like a delicious delirium in his veins.

On first reading this passage, you might be tempted to regard it as a simple description of a boy-girl romantic moment. It is late in the evening; they do not want to part; they are presumably 'in love' and so they wander through the wood, sharing together the beauty of the place and their feelings for each other. But, is this just romance? Is it adequate to describe Paul and Miriam as being 'in love' and leave the question of their relationship at that? One might have expected them to kiss but they do not do so despite the moment of intense intimacy before the roses. Nor are they in perfect harmony although they find themselves in almost perfect surroundings. Consider who takes the initiative in this passage. Notice the references to Paul's anxiety. To whom does the experience mean most? It is clear that their relationship is far more complex than one might at first have supposed.

In writing answers to the following questions, you need to be fully aware of the different emotional states of Paul and Miriam at various points during this incident. The reactions with which we are faced are clues to Lawrence's overall conception of the relationship. In order to sharpen our sensitivity to these clues and so to appreciate more of the quality of their relationship, we need to look very closely at what the author says directly about their feelings — 'she was pale and expectant', or 'he listened, vaguely anxious' — and at what they say to each other. Then there are a number of minor but very telling details of response, the one to the other or to the natural things about them, such as Paul's slow, almost reluctant, following of Miriam into the wood, his concern about the family that grumble if he is late arriving home, his uncertainty about the 'whiteness' that might be a patch of fog or a cloud of flowers: he is not certain of what the situation means, not giving himself wholly into it. In addition, we need to be aware that Lawrence describes the rose bush and other aspects of nature in such a way as to suggest the various feelings that the characters have towards these natural beauties. For example, Paul describes the roses, after he has turned aside from his too intense, silent communion with Miriam, and his description compares them with butterflies, something living, natural and moving. It is as if he needs to bring them down to earth. Whilst appreciating the beauty of the bush, he does not want to be wholly absorbed into Miriam's worship and spiritual intensity. She, on the other hand, wants to become utterly identified with what is for her a very holy thing: she goes forward impulsively and touches the flowers. He tries to make the moment more ordinary; she tries to intensify the feelings of wonder and worship. So, when she looks at the roses, Lawrence describes them as 'holy' or 'expanded in ecstasy'. Similarly, when they have parted, Paul 'stumbled down the path'. He is still in the wood, where he cannot breathe, being almost suffocated by anxious imprisonment in feelings that are too intense for him. But, when he comes to the meadow, Lawrence describes it as 'free' and 'open' and there Paul is able to enjoy the relief of vigorous physical exercise, of ordinary physical exertion.

Having read the passage carefully, and pondered over the sort of details in it to which I have been directing your attention, write answers to the following questions. You will find suggested answers on page 209?

1. Examine the first 23 lines of this extract. What feeling do Paul and Miriam have in common? How do their feelings and concerns differ?

2. Explain in your own words why Miriam wants to show Paul the wild rose-bush (lines 31–4).

3. (a) Why does Paul turn away from Miriam 'as if pained' in line 81?
   (b) What other indications are there in the section from line 40 to line 94 that there is some conflict of feelings in Paul?

(c) Why do you think he breaks into a run as soon as he is out of the wood?

4. How do Paul and Miriam differ in their reactions to the roses?

5. Comment on the meaning and effectiveness of the following phrases or sentences:
'Only he could make it her own, immortal,' (lines 33–4);
'splashing the darkness everywhere with great split stars' (lines 68–9);
'His look seemed to travel down into her,' (line 79);
'a white, virgin scent,' (line 92);
'like a delicious delirium in his veins.' (lines 100–1).

6. Finally, write a short paragraph which summarises your understanding of the relationship between Paul and Miriam.

To conclude this chapter, which has been concerned with the development of your understanding of people in books, I include another passage which presents two people in love but this time, there is no introduction or commentary. Read it carefully – it is from a novel by Colette called *Ripening Seed* – and then write answers to the questions. Before you embark on the passage, it would be helpful for you to look over the summary of key points and rules with which the chapter finishes. When you compare your final answers with the suggested answers on page 210, you will be able to gauge the extent to which you have developed those skills of detailed, sensitive reading, appreciation of characters and understanding of their relationships in books that I have been stressing.

Vinca sighed, and opened her eyes again without raising her head.

"I'm not tiring you, am I, Phil?"

5

He shook his head and gazed with admiration into her eyes, whose blue, each time more dear to his heart, flickered elusive between their fair-tipped lashes.

10 "Look out there," he said. "The storm is already dying down. There'll be another huge tide at four in the morning . . . But we can trust that rift and expect a lovely full moonrise tonight."

Instinctively he spoke of smooth seas and halcyon skies, to
15 guide her thoughts towards serener images, but she gave no
sign of response.

"You're coming to play tennis at the Jallons' tomorrow?"

20 She shut her eyes and shook her head in sudden fury, as
though refusing to eat or drink, or even to go on living.

"Vinca, you must!" Philippe was stern in his insistence.
"We'll have to go."
25

Her lips parted and her eyes gazed searchingly out to sea, like
those of a prisoner under sentence of death.

"We'll have to go, then," she repeated. "But what's the use of
30 going? What's the use of not going? Nothing makes any
difference."

The thoughts of both turned to the Jallons' garden, to tea and
tennis. They thought, in the purity of their frenzied love, of
35 the game they must play, for yet another tomorrow, in the
guise of laughing children, and both felt worn out with
fatigue.

"Only a few more days and we'll be parted" – Philippe again
40 took up the burden of his thoughts. "We'll no longer wake up
under the same roof, and I shan't see Vinca except on
Sundays, either at home, or at her father's, or at the movies.
And I'm sixteen! Sixteen and five make twenty-one.
Hundreds and hundreds of days . . . A few months in the hols,
45 it's true; but then their last few days are always nightmarish.
And to think she belongs to me? That she's mine!"

It was then that he noticed Vinca slowly slipping away from
his shoulder. With eyes tight shut, she was slipping quietly,
50 imperceptibly, deliberately, down the slope of the rocky
ledge, so narrow, that her feet were already dangling over
space . . . He grasped the situation and felt no fear. He
deliberated on the timelessness of her action, then tightened
his arm around her waist so as never to be parted from her. As
55 he pressed Vinca close, he was conscious of the full living
reality, resilience, and vigorous perfection of her young body,
ready to obey him in life, ready to drag him down with her to
death . . .

"Death! But what's the use of dying? ... Not yet. Must I go
down to the nether world without having really possessed all
this, this girl who was born to be mine?"

On that sloping rock he dreamed of possession as a timid
youth might dream, but also as an exacting man, as an
inheritor grimly resolved to enjoy the fruits appointed him by
time and the laws of man. For the first time it was for him to
decide the fate of their future as lovers, and, as master of that
fate, to choose whether to abandon her to the waves or plant
her firmly on that jut of rock, like the stubborn seeds that
flourished there with so little encouragement.

Tightening his arms around her like a belt, he hoisted up the
graceful young body so heavy to hold, and woke her by
calling out a brief "Come along now, Vinca!"

She gazed up at him as he stood over her, and seeing him
firmly resolute and impatient, it dawned on her that the hour
of dying was over. With rapturous indignation she found the
setting sun reflected in Phil's dark eyes, on his ruffled hair, on
his mouth, and on the shadow in the shape of two small wings
of virile down above it, and she cried out, "You don't love me
enough, Phil, you don't love me enough!"

1. Exactly where are these two characters during the course of
   this extract?

2. Describe Vinca's mood at the opening of this passage (lines 1
   to 16).

3. Why does Philippe talk about the sea and the moonrise to
   Vinca (line 10)?

4. Distinguish carefully between the different attitudes of
   Philippe and Vinca towards the Jallons' tea party.

5. Describe in your own words how they see themselves
   behaving at the Jallons'.

6. What are Philippe's thoughts about the future (lines 39–46)?

7. When Vinca starts slipping off the ledge, what does the action signify both to her and to Philippe? (You should refer to two different points in the passage.)

8. Why does Philippe feel no fear when she starts slipping down?

9. (a) What alternatives for action present themselves to Philippe in lines 66–70?
   (b) What makes him decide to act as he does?

10. Why do you think Vinca accuses Philippe of not loving her enough?

11. Explain the meaning of the following phrases by relating them carefully to the context in which they appear:
   'like those of a prisoner under sentence of death,' (line 27);
   'in the purity of their frenzied love,' (line 34);
   'but also as an exacting man,' (line 64);
   'With rapturous indignation' (line 78).

Summary of key points and rules in chapter 2

1. Read the passage more than once, making absolutely sure that you have not skimmed over any details of description. The writer intends you to read everything.

2. A novelist uses situations in order to reveal something about his characters. As you read through even a short extract, therefore, notice how your sense of the personalities of the characters fills out and develops.

3. The relationships that a novelist creates in his books are rarely static: they develop just as characters develop and are modified by particular circumstances. When you read an extract which deals with relationships between people, notice how the situation affects the relationship.

4. Understanding people in books is not merely a matter of collecting evidence about them in a clinical manner. Let your feelings guide you into a sympathetic understanding. Try to appreciate what they might be feeling and how their feelings would be changing from moment to moment.

5. In writing answers to comprehension questions, it is important to answer as relevantly and precisely as possible. Do not refer to material in the passage which does not directly answer the question but always include all the evidence which is relevant.

Chapter 3
Appreciating Descriptions

The writer's intentions

In the Ordinary-level English Language papers, the examiners invariably want to test candidates' capacities to appreciate and understand a variety of passages, which may contain different sorts of vocabulary and have been written for different purposes. Consider for a moment the range of possible intentions behind any one piece of writing; the author may want to entertain or to amuse, to deepen his readers' appreciation of the complexities of other people, to share personal experiences and memories, to provoke an imaginative response, to inform the reader or to make him think. The list of possible intentions or combinations of these aims is almost endlessly varied and complex. So too is the range of audiences for which an author may write: if he is a scholar, he may be producing a learned article which will be read by a handful of specialist students; if he is a journalist, he may be read by a mass audience drawn from a particular social class with a common political outlook. He must temper his vocabulary and ideas according to his expected readership and their manner of reading.

The different intentions of the scholar and journalist are quite obvious and the reader would swiftly identify these writers' aims and read in an appropriate manner. Similarly, you would have little difficulty in distinguishing the different types of attention required of you when settling down to read a book on car maintenance, on the one hand, or a novel about racing drivers, on the other. However, there are many modes of writing which fall between these obvious extremes and which therefore require more subtle adjustments of attention from the reader. I include some examples of such writing in this chapter.

If you have the capacity for swiftly adjusting to the passage before you and sensing the intentions of the writer, and therefore the sort of attention you will have to give to the passage, you will certainly be all the more able to deal with whatever is printed on your examination paper. The more subtly you can perceive the writer's intentions, the more intelligently you will read what he has written.

As a starting point, I shall draw a broad distinction between the intentions behind the passages in the last chapter and those which follow in this chapter and, as we work through the descriptions that follow, I shall be pointing out what you should be looking for in order to develop your sensitivity to the range of intentions that a writer may have.

All the passages in the last chapter were taken from novels and we were mainly concerned with understanding some of the ways in which fictional characters are created and developed by novelists. Most novels are entirely fictional worlds. The novelist is bound all the time to use bits of 'real life', to include memories of things seen or done by himself or others and to base his descriptions, to a greater or lesser extent, on places and people he has known, but the overriding intention of most novels is to create the sense of a world complete in itself, a world which has its origin and birth in the mind of the novelist and not in the real world outside.

In this chapter, we shall be considering writing which is not fictional but which nevertheless does have an imaginative element in it. These passages of description and explanation are all taken from books whose authors were primarily concerned to describe and explain the real world around them as they saw it. The intention here is not so much to create the separate and unified world of a novel as to extend the reader's appreciation of the infinite variety of men and things around us, sometimes to make us feel or think in a particular way about what is being described. It is, of course, true that a novelist may on occasions do the same thing and that these distinctions of 'fact' and 'fiction' are in some ways artificial. However, all the books from which the llowing passages are taken present themselves as factual accounts. The intentions behind them vary considerably, as we shall see.

To extend the reader's experience

An autobiography

We shall start by looking closely at a passage taken from Edwin Muir's *An Autobiography* and we shall examine it in such a way as to isolate the various intentions of the author, which are combined in this book to create a life-story of unusual power and variety. This should help you to appreciate more fully how a writer's intentions can be understood by the reader. Once you have established a sense of these intentions, you will have a framework within which you

· can pay attention to details and answer precise questions without a disturbing feeling that the passage as a whole does not mean anything to you.

The early chapters of Muir's *An Autobiography* describe his childhood in a remote Orkney island. They contain a great deal of detail about how the people there lived, what work they did, their houses, their religion, their food, the patterns of their days and the main events in the yearly cycle of life. It gives us, in fact, an insight into a society and a way of life which is very different from nearly all the societies existing today in the United Kingdom, since even the remoter parts of present-day Britain are not quite as isolated and self-supporting as were the Orkneys in the early part of this century. So we may say that one of the intentions of this author is to interest us in a way of life of which few of us can have had any direct experience. One of his aims is to extend our knowledge of the world and of possible ways of life. In the following extract, for example, we are given much information about the customs of eating at that time in the Orkneys, the diet of the people, the way in which food was preserved and kept, the extent to which this society was self-supporting, the part played on the island of Wyre by the shopkeeper and the importance of the Lammas Market, 'the great yearly event'.

If this material were all that were present in the book, we could regard it as a 'sociological description': the book could be defined quite simply as an informed and imaginative account of the way a particular society functioned. But there is more to it than that. Read the following passage through several times and note down in writing everything that does *not* directly contribute to a picture of a society, that is, everything which suggests that the author wants to do more than simply convey information about another society. When you have made a list in this way, read the commentary that follows the passage.

We always returned from church to a good dinner of soup with a chicken, or, as we called it, more honestly, a hen, cooked in it, followed by "spotted dog". Now that my sailor suit has come back again I find that it is associated with these
5   Sunday dinners and the shining spoons and knives and forks laid out on the white tablecloth. During the week we did not bother much about knives and forks and tablecloths. A big plate of herring or other fish was set in the middle of the table,

41

along with a dish of potatoes, and we simply stretched out our
hands. The traditional Orkney invitation to a visitor was,
"Put in thee hand," though when a visitor appeared knives
and forks were usually laid out. We hardly ever ate meat or
fowl more than once a week. It was the same at all the other
farms, and nobody seemed to be the worse for it. Our supper
was porridge. The porridge-pot was set down in the middle of
the floor, and we all sat round it with great bowls of milk and
ladled the porridge into the milk.

Our diet was a curious one by town standards. We went
without many necessaries, or what are considered necessaries
– beef, for instance – and had a great number of luxuries
which we did not know to be luxuries, such as plovers' eggs,
trout, crab, and lobster: I ate so much crab and lobster as a boy
that I have never been able to enjoy them since. Our staples
were homemade oat bannocks and barley bannocks, butter,
eggs, and homemade cheese, which we had in abundance;
white bread, bought at the Wyre shop, was looked upon as a
luxury. In the kitchen, there was a big girnel with a sliding
top; inside it was divided into two, one compartment being
filled with oat-meal and the other with barley-meal. The meal
had to be pressed firmly down, otherwise it would not keep.
The girnel, when the top was slid aside, gave out a thick,
sleepy smell which seemed to go to my head and make me
drowsy. It was connected with a nightmare which I often
had, in which my body seemed to swell to a great size and
then slowly dwindle again, while the drowsy smell of meal
filled my nostrils. It is from smell that we get our most intense
realisation of the solidity of things. The smell of the meal
pressed tightly down in the girnel made me realise its *mass*.
though I could see only its surface, which was smooth and
looked quite shallow. My nightmares probably came from an
apprehension of the mere bulk of life, the feeling that the
world is so crammed with solid, bulging objects that there is
not enough room for all of them . . .

Our life at the Bu was virtually self-supporting. The pig, after
being slaughtered each year, was cut up and salted, and the
pork stored away in a barrel. I helped with the salting when I
was quite small, and got a sense of pleased importance from
rubbing the raw slices of meat on coarse salt strewn on a
wooden board: these neat cubes did not seem to have any
connexion with the butchered pig. We had fish almost as

often as we wanted it, and crabs when Sutherland went to lift
his creels; and Aunt Maggie was often down on the beach
55 gathering whelks. The oat bannocks and barley bannocks, the
milk, butter, cheese, and eggs, were our own produce. We
sent part of the wool after the sheep-shearing down to a
Border town, and it came back as blankets and cloth. We
bought at the shop such things as white bread, sugar, tea,
60 treacle, currants and raisins, and paraffin oil for the lamps.

Old Fred of the shop was a very genteel man with an accent
which he had picked up in his young days while serving in a
grocery store in Edinburgh. He was the only man on the
65 island who shaved and put on a collar every day, and this set
him apart from other men as a sort of priest smelling
perpetually of the clean odours of tea, tobacco, and paraffin
oil. He emphasised the difference by wearing a straw hat,
summer and winter, both outside and inside the shop. Having
70 seen the world, he looked down on us for our insularity, and
showed that he thought his Edinburgh manners, suitable for a
fine Princes Street shop, were cast away on us islanders. He
was a thin, sensitive little man, terribly proper: a gentle
bachelor with pernickety ways. He is long since dead.
75

The Lammas market was the great yearly event. It was held
in Kirkwall, but though my father and my older brother and
sisters usually went to it, I was never taken, for the journey
was considered too long and tiring. On the first Monday of
80 the market, the Fawn, which plied between Rousay and
Kirkwall, stopped a little distance out from Wyre – for there
was no pier – and someone rowed out the people who wanted
to go to the market. I cannot recollect my family ever setting
out, but I remember clearly my brother and sisters returning
85 from it one year. I had bronchitis and was not allowed
outside; but when they came in sight my mother let me go to
the end of the house and watch them coming. I can see them
still passing the corner of the ruined chapel; they were all in
their best clothes; it was a still, warm summer evening. They
90 bought presents for me, pink sweets I had never seen before,
ribbed like snowdrifts, rough chunks of yellow rock, and new,
dark brown, smooth sweets which I did not much care for:
chocolates. I had expected a jumping-jack as well, for my
mother had often described one to me which had once been in
95 the house; but no jumping-jacks could be had at the market;
they were out of fashion, and I had to put up instead with a

large wooden egg, out of which a snake shot, rustling, when you opened it. I never had many toys, and never got much genuine satisfaction from them: the enjoyment was conscious
100 make-believe with an undercurrent of disappointment: I always expected every toy to do more than it could do.

Look now at your list of material from this passage which does not fall into the category of 'sociological description'. It should begin with the author's reference to his sailor suit, which he had, in fact, discovered many years after the life he is here describing, and which recalled to him the memory of the Sunday dinners of his childhood. Another item in your list is likely to be the author's reference to his having eaten so much crab and lobster as a boy that he has been unable to enjoy them since. These two simple observations indicate several aspects of the writing which we must be aware of if we are to fully respond to the passage.

First of all, the description is personal: it concerns the author's own childhood and we see the people and events he describes largely through the eyes of a child. Muir is not a social scientist describing a remote life-style in an entirely objective way, for his presence, as he was as a child, in the narrative suggests personal feelings and associations. All the description is somehow coated with this personal feeling. Secondly, we must recognise, too, the presence of the author as he is at the time of writing. The book is not simply a description of something that happened long ago: the author is constantly relating what he was as a boy to what he is now and is showing how his earliest experiences contributed to the make-up of his present personality and tastes.

You may also have noted down the reference to foods which are usually considered to be 'necessaries' and the description of other foods as 'luxuries', although the islanders did not know them to be luxuries. At this point, the author is making judgements about the life-style of the islanders from the point of view of a modern town or mainland dweller. He is referring to the average tastes and standards of the town dweller in order to contrast our estimate of things with that of the islanders.

The presence of the author as a mature man, able to look back and to estimate the importance of his childhood in forming his tastes and ways of looking at life, is a sort of subterranean current running through this description and occasionally reaching the surface with considerable force. This happens towards the end of the second paragraph, where Muir describes how, as a small child, he reacted to looking into and smelling the great barrel of meal that was kept in the family kitchen. The meal gave off a 'thick, sleepy smell' which he always associated with a particular nightmare he often had. The nightmare seems to have been an exploration of his own sense of size in relation to the world about him and to express the fear of being overwhelmed. We cannot be exactly sure of its significance but Edwin Muir goes on to suggest an interpretation which might explain why such a nightmare arose out of his experience of smelling the meal. He is, at this point in his description, standing outside the events and memories he is narrating and making sense of them.

I want to emphasise this simple point: the author is present in his book, commenting on his descriptions of facts, feelings and events of the past. His intention cannot, therefore, be limited to the aim of conveying the quality of life in a remote Orkney island, nor simply to the describing of various feelings that he had as a child. One of his intentions is to understand and explain the connections between the life into which he was born, the environment about him, and the person that he was within himself. So, as well as having your experience extended through imagination, you are being invited to think about the way his childhood affected him, the way in which he grew up.

The last paragraph contains another example of the adult writer explaining the feelings and experience of the child that he once was. He writes about a toy that was given him and about the feeling of disappointment he had when he played with it. As a child, he would not have been able to explain that feeling but, as an adult, he is able to put the matter neatly into perspective and say that he 'always expected every toy to be able to do more than it could do'.

Your list of material that is not simply description of the society in general terms probably contains two other references that I would like to comment on. They again show the different points of view through which we are invited to see Edwin Muir's childhood. In the last paragraph, we see, through the eyes of the child, his brother and sisters returning on one occasion from the Lammas market, in their best clothes, on a warm summer's evening. This description evokes feelings in us about the child, his confinement in the house and the contrast between his rather lonely, sickly, small life and the brighter, more outgoing and expansive world of his older brother and sisters, who, we may presume, were excited and cheerful after the great event of the market. If we are reading closely, we will, through imagination, identify with the child and 'feel for him'.

We are invited to appreciate, from a rather different standpoint, the portrait of 'Old Fred of the shop'. This contains a precise summary of a man's tastes and attitudes and personality that only a mature writer could possibly have written. Edwin Muir sees him from a distance and reminds us that it is from a distance in the last sentence of that paragraph: 'He is long since dead.' Because he views from a distance, he can see the chief characteristics of the man all the more clearly and can suggest how he fitted into the society on the island and his relationship with the islanders. These two short passages of description are very different in their effects; the return from the market produces a feeling of immediacy and sympathy and the portrait of Old Fred induces a more distant, detached assessment. Yet they both suggest a similar sense of sadness, a sort of humane tenderness for people, and this feeling runs through most of Edwin Muir's book and gives a unity to much varied material.

I have said enough now for you to realise that, even in the most apparently straightforward piece of descriptive writing, there are undercurrents and intentions that may not be immediately obvious. Keep a lively mind when you are dealing with this sort of writing and ask yourself continually what you think the writer's intentions are. They may not be as simple as first appears.

The following questions are of the type that has been recently set by a number of examination boards on this sort of passage. Some of them require the candidate to comment closely on the introduction nd development of lines of thought or of associations; others ask for commentary on the 'nuances' or underlying meanings of words and phrases. Some questions require you to summarise information and the last two questions require you to distinguish between the different sorts of material included in the passage. When you come to answer questions 10 and 11, you will find it helpful to look back and re-read my introduction to the passage and the commentary that follows it. Write out answers to the questions and, when you have finished, compare your answers with the suggestions on page 211.

1. In what two ways was the Sunday dinner different from weekday meals?

2. What thought is added by the author's inclusion of the phrase, 'more honestly' (line 2)?

3. What idea has the writer introduced into the first paragraph by the statement, 'nobody seemed to be the worse for it' (line 14)?

4. Upon what information and ideas contained in the second paragraph does the following sentence comment:
   'It is from smell that we get our most intense realisation of the solidity of things'?

   Answer this question in about three sentences.

5. What information given in the third paragraph justifies the author's use of the word 'virtually' in line 46?

6. What is implied about the child's feelings in the statement:
   'these neat cubes did not seem to have any connexion with the butchered pig'?

7. Edwin Muir describes Old Fred as being set 'apart from other men as a sort of priest'. What information in the fourth paragraph supports this description?

   Answer this question in about four sentences.

8. (a) Which statement in the fourth paragraph summarises the author's estimate of Old Fred's character?
   (b) How do you suppose this adult estimate differs from the author's childhood view of the man?

9. 'the enjoyment was conscious make-believe with an undercurrent of disappointment' (lines 99–100)
   (a) What does the word 'conscious' add to this statement?
   (b) Why does the writer describe his disappointment as an 'undercurrent'?
   (c) What else in the last paragraph suggests melancholy and gisappointment?

10. Consider the whole passage and then make a series of general statements which summarise the information which is given us about the way of life on the island of Wyre?

11. Which memories give us a sense of the sort of child the author was? What do we learn about his characteristic childhood feelings?

Into Spain

We have examined a passage which contains different types of statement, ranging from the very personal to the quite objective and impersonal. Edwin Muir's writing is calm and ordered and, at every point, he moves towards creating a more precise understanding in the reader. This understanding is closely related to our feeling that he has worked through his past experiences in his mind and has arrived at a state of maturity from which he can look back calmly and see how they fall into a pattern. He may describe something that was, at the time, quite terrifying, like his nightmares, but because he can now see what they meant for him, how they were caused, and can summarise his understanding in a statement like, 'My nightmares probably came from an apprehension of the mere bulk of life', these events no longer seem terrifying; they have been defused. The feelings that overwhelmed him in the past, when he was a small boy, have been changed into calm understanding.

The passage we are now going to consider is very different. It is also taken from an autobiographical work – *As I Walked Out One Midsummer Morning* by Laurie Lee – and it describes the author's experience as a young man travelling on foot through Spain. Read through the passage below several times. It concerns Laurie Lee's first encounter with a Spanish village shortly after arriving in the country. After you have read it and enjoyed it, ask yourself these questions:

1. What seems particularly dramatic and strange in this passage?
2. At which points are you most aware of the author responding to the situation around him?
3. Is the author more or less present in the scene of the story than was Edwin Muir in his autobiography?
4. Would you say that this passage moves towards abstract statements in the same way as the previous passage?
5. Does the reader come closer to actually experiencing the events, seeing and hearing them in his imagination, than he did in the previous passage?

. Do not worry if you cannot answer these questions thoroughly but do think along these general lines whilst reading the passage. Try to grasp the overall intentions of the writer and summarise what he is offering his readers.

Then I remember coming out of a gorge one early evening and seeing my first real village. I remember it well, because it was like all Spain, and it was also my first encounter. It stood on a bare brown rock in the sinking sun – a pile of squat
5 houses like cubes of pink sugar. In the centre rose a tower from which a great black bell sent out cracked jerking gusts of vibration. I'd had enough of the hills and lying around in wet bracken, and now I smelt fires and a sweet tang of cooking. I climbed the steep road into the village, and black-robed
10 women, standing in doorways, made soft exclamations as I went by.

In the village square I came on a great studded door bearing the sign: "Posada de Nuestra Señora." I pushed the door
15 open and entered a whitewashed courtyard hanging with geraniums and crowded with mules and asses. There was bedlam in the courtyard – mules stamping, asses braying, chickens cackling and children fighting. A fat old crone, crouching by a fire in the corner, was stirring soup in a large
20 black cauldron, and as she seemed to be in charge I went up to her and made a sign for food. Without a word she lifted a ladleful of the soup and held it up to my mouth. I tasted and choked; it was hot, strong and acrid with smoke and herbs. The old lady peered at me sharply through the fumes of the
25 fire. She was bent, leather-skinned, bearded and fanged, and looked like a watchful moose. I wiped my burnt mouth, nodded my head, and said "Good" in clear loud English. She took a long pull herself, her moustached lips working, her eyes rolling back in her skull. Then she spat briskly into the
30 fire, turned her head abruptly and roared out in a deep, hoarse voice – and a barefooted boy, dressed only in a shirt, came and tugged my sleeve and led me to see the bedrooms.

Later I was sitting in the courtyard under the swinging
35 light-bulbs, hungrily watching the supper cooking, when the innkeeper came out, a towel round his waist, and began to scrub his young son in the horse-trough. The infant screamed, the old crone roared, the father shouted, sang and lathered. Then, suddenly, as by a whim, he shoved the child under the

40 water and left him to see what he'd do. The screams were cut
off as though by a knife, while the old woman and the father
watched him. In a fierce, choking silence the child fought the
water, kicking and struggling like a small brown frog, eyes
open, mouth working, his whole body grappling with the
45 sudden inexplicable threat of death. He was about one year
old, but for a moment seemed ageless, facing terror alone and
dumb. Then just as he was about to give in, the woman picked
up a bucket and threw it at the father's head, and at that he
snatched up the child, tossed him in the air, smothered him
50 with kisses and carried him away.

Supper was laid at last on the long wooden table set out under
the open sky. When it was ready the innkeeper, with a sweep
of his arm, invited me to join them. Carters and drovers
55 gathered quickly round the table, and a girl dealt out loaves to
each of us, and we ate the stew from a common dish, scooping
it up with our bread. The old woman sat beside me and roared
at me continuously, pinching my legs and thumping me in the
belly and urging me on to eat.
60
Half-way through supper we were joined by two shifty-eyed
men who came in carrying a new-skinned lamb. They looked
starved, desperate and poor as dogs, and their shirts hung in
rags from their shoulders. They approached us in silence and
65 nobody greeted them, nor did they seem to expect it. They
dropped the bleeding lamb at the far end of the table, threw
themselves down and called for wine. Then they began to tear
at the carcass, cramming the meat in their mouths and darting
fugitive looks over their shoulders. Their movements had all
70 the sharp snapping nervousness of beasts at a kill, crouching
low and cracking the bones with their teeth. When the girl
had brought them their wine, they were left to themselves —
their meal was their own secret business.

75 At our end of the table, supper was prolonged and noisy, and I
didn't know whether it was night or morning. By now I was
gorged with stew and warmed to idiocy by wine; I was the
stranger, but I felt at home. In each face around me I seemed
to recognise characters from my own village: the carters,
80 innkeepers, the dust-covered farmboys, grandmothers and
girls, they were all here. I felt like a child crawling on the edge
of some rousing family life which I had yet to grow to
understand. And I think they felt it too, for they treated me

like a child – grinning, shouting, acting dumb-shows to please
85 me and smoothing my way with continual tit-bits and
indulgences.

At last supper was over. The women swept the dishes away,
and the carters curled up on the ground to sleep. The two
90 outcasts lay snoring across their end of the table, their faces
buried in a debris of bones. I rose from my chair and stumbled
away to my room, where I found six beds, full of men and
fleas. Fowls were roosting in the rafters, and an old man lay
fully clothed on the floor, fast asleep, with a goat tethered to
95 his ankle. The room was stifling, but the straw bed was soft.
And there I slept, my head roaring with Spain.

That was just one night, an early one on my journey, and also
my first inn, like many others to come. From then on the days
100 merged into a continuous movement of sun and shadow,
hunger and thirst, fatigue and sleep, all fused and welded into
one coloured mass by the violent heat of that Spanish
summer.

Having read through the passage carefully and thought over the
general questions that preceded it, you should now have some idea
of the writer's intentions, of what sort of experience he is offering
the reader. Like Edwin Muir, Laurie Lee is exposing us to a glimpse
of a way of life far removed from our own. We are unlikely to have
been as adventurous as he was in exploring continental countries
on foot, and so he is giving us the opportunity of an imaginative
journey in his company, through a land whose atmosphere and
people he vividly recreates in his writing. This Spanish village and
its inn are alive and immediate; sights and smells and sounds are
strikingly present.

It would, I think, be true to say that Muir's account of the Orkney
society is more 'distanced', more a general explanation of the way
the society worked than Laurie Lee's description of the Spanish
village. Whereas Muir talks about what used to happen at meal
times, Lee recreates dramatically a particular occasion, giving us
the story of one sequence of events on one particular evening.
There is less explanation and background and more evocative
detail in this second passage. This does not at all imply that one
passage is better than the other but simply shows that they are
different and consequently make different demands on the reader.
It should perhaps be mentioned that, although Lee makes this

51

evening seem unique and particular, something that happened once and all on the same occasion, he also says that the village is memorable because 'it was like all Spain', and that the inn was 'like many others to come'. It was typical as well as being unique. We might quite reasonably suppose that some of the details have been taken from memories of other occasions and included in the story to give it more life and richness.

We can make one other direct comparison with the earlier passage from Muir's autobiography. Like him, Laurie Lee is present in his narrative and is part of the action. The reaction of the villagers to him is noted carefully, for example, the 'soft exclamations' of the Spanish women as he passes them. The phrase suggests their politely muted surprise and, also, their approval because he is, after all, young and fresh and different in appearance from the Spanish men. Lee does not perhaps dwell on his feelings quite as much as Muir and we must wonder exactly what he does feel when he encounters the old woman or sees the father shoving his child under the water. That is an extraordinary moment in the narrative and the author heightens it by making a general statement about what the child was enduring: 'He was about one year old, but for a moment seemed ageless, facing terror alone and dumb.' This invites the reader to react to the incident but does not directly indicate what the author's feelings were. Part of the pleasure of reading a piece like this comes from imagining what we would have felt in those circumstances and how we would have reacted. The author's reticence about his responses enable the reader's responses to arise more readily. In a similar way, we are left to do our own thinking about the two 'shifty-eyed men', who are in some sense social outcasts though tolerated to the extent of being allowed to eat their meal in the inn and buy wine.

However, towards the end of this extract, the author gives us a perfectly contrived insight into the way he was fitting in with the ople at the inn. As the food and wine took their effect and he relaxed with the company, he began to feel 'at home' and yet, at the same time, he was the stranger and so could not be completely at one with them. This curious feeling is precisely conveyed in the comparison of himself to a child who is part of the family and as yet unable to know himself in this role or to understand all that is going on around him.

As I have already implied, this passage is rich in its descriptive effects and written with great precision. It is therefore to be expected that the questions asked on it will include a number which relate closely to the meanings and associations of particular words and phrases. Always keep in mind that this is not a bald piece of objective description, divorced from all feeling. Much of the feeling in the passage is not stated openly but subtly suggested in the choice of descriptive words and phrases. Read the passage through, responding to it again as fully as you can and then answer the following questions. Suggested answers may be found on page 212 but do not refer to them until you have completed your own answers.

1. Put into your own words the **two** reasons the author gives for his clear memory of this village.

2. 'like cubes of pink sugar' (line 5)
   What details and associations are added to the description by this phrase?

3. What does the word 'jerking' add to the description of the tolling bell (line 6)?

4. What does 'soft exclamations' (line 10) suggest about the way the Spanish women reacted to the author?

5. Why do you think the author says ' "Good" in clear loud English' on tasting the soup?

6. (a) For what reason is it appropriate for the struggling child to be described as 'a small brown frog' (line 43)?
   (b) What ideas does the following phrase add to the passage: 'but for a moment seemed ageless'?
   (c) Is there any evidence to suggest that the father was not being consciously cruel to his son?

7. What details in the fifth paragraph show that the 'two shifty-eyed men' were (a) tolerated by the company and (b) not approved of?

8. Which statement in the fifth paragraph summarises the author's ideas about the nature of the two men's meal?

9. Using only material from line 75–86, write a summary in your

own words recording all that we are told of the author's **thoughts** and **feelings**.

10. Summarise the actions of the old lady throughout the extract and say what attitude towards the author she seems to be displaying.

11. What meaning would have been lost had the author omitted the phrase, 'my head roaring with Spain' (line 96)?

12. Write down three short statements which identify the three ideas or facts combined in the final sentence in this extract.

To make the reader think

We have, so far in this chapter, looked at two passages from books written primarily to entertain the reader by extending his experience through imagination. We may not have had the opportunity to go to Spain at all and it is unlikely that we have travelled there in the way Laurie Lee did, but, as we read through *As I Walked Out One Midsummer Morning*, we are given the pleasure of experiencing the land and the people and of losing ourselves in the adventures that befell the author. Edwin Muir's book is more complex but, like Lee, he opens up his life and thoughts to us, inviting us to take from them whatever interest or pleasure we can. Neither of these writers is concerned to convince us of anything or to make us change our ideas, though, of course, it is open to us to allow ourselves to be influenced by the authors' experiences and ideas if they happen to appeal to us.

Much descriptive writing has, however, a more clear-cut aim in which the writer is trying to convey ideas or attitudes to us and to convince us that at least they have something to say for them and that they are probably right. Such a writer, out to influence our minds, change our attitudes, or convince us of the validity of an argument, will use description in his books in a different way and for different purposes from its use in the books we have looked at.

The neighbourhood
In commenting on Edwin Muir's *An Autobiography*, I distinguished it from a 'sociological description', that is, a description which is presented to us so that we may come to understand how a

society functions, what makes it tick, how the different parts of the society fit together, the common assumptions that are shared by the people in that society, and so on. We shall proceed now to consider just such a piece of description. It is taken from *The Uses of Literacy* by Richard Hoggart, a book that has, incidentally, provided a number of comprehension passages for examination papers in recent years.

This book is about changing patterns of literacy and reading habits, about what the mass of people read and the extent to which popular literature is related to the life and values of the people for whom it is produced. The early part of the book is largely a description of the way a working-class community in the north of England would have functioned when the author was a boy. He is able to draw on his own experience as a working-class boy and to portray in vivid detail the assumptions, morals and social relationships that he remembers and to recreate a sense of the day-to-day life of such a community.

In contrast to Edwin Muir, Hoggart is not concerned that the reader should understand the author and how his early experiences affected him. The description of working-class life is rather the data which he analyses and from which he draws various points, out of which an argument is created.

When you are faced with an extract from this sort of book, you need to become aware of the part that the descriptive passages are playing in building up the sequence of insights or points, out of which the author will develop his ideas and arguments. Very often, such a writer will make a general statement and then elaborate or demonstrate his assertion by producing descriptive evidence. At other times, the descriptive material will be so ordered that the author is able to produce a statement which summarises or interprets what he has been describing.

Hoggart's book does not, therefore, contain anecdotes unless they are relevant to the point he is making, whereas Muir's book, as we noticed, frequently moves by anecdotes, one remembered incident recalling a feeling, which, in turn, recalls another incident, and so on. The process whereby Muir develops his book is one of **association**; Hoggart's book develops by **ideas**, by **logic**.

Questions set on passages like the one that follows will probably require you to demonstrate that you grasp the relevance of the description to the ideas that run through the writing. Very often the description is 'loaded' so as to indicate a particular judgement or attitude to what is being described and so you may be asked to examine particular phrases so as to determine what attitude is being suggested in the choice of descriptive words. You may also have to show what evidence is being used by the author to support a general statement or state concisely an idea which is being elaborated in the description.

When you have read the following passage and completed your written answers to the questions, read the commentary that comes after the questions and see if you can improve your answers, before consulting the suggested answers on page 214.

Home may be private, but the front door opens out of the living-room on to the street, and when you go down the one step or use it as a seat on a warm evening you become part of the life of the neighbourhood.

5

To a visitor they are understandably depressing, these massed proletarian areas; street after regular street of shoddily uniform houses intersected by a dark pattern of ginnels and snickets (alley-ways) and courts; mean, squalid, and in a
10 permanent half-fog; a study in shades of dirty-grey, without greenness or the blueness of sky; degrees darker than the north or west of the town, than the "better end". The brickwork and the woodwork are cheap; the wood goes too long between repaintings – landlords are not as anxious to
15 keep up the value of the property as are owner-occupiers. The nearest park or green open space is some distance away, but the terraces are gap-toothed with sour and brick-bespattered bits of waste-ground and there is a piece of free ground half a mile away, called "t' Moor". Evocative name: it is a clinkered
20 six-acre stretch surrounded by works and grimy pubs, with a large red-brick urinal at its edge.

The houses are fitted into the dark and lowering canyons between the giant factories and the services which attend
25 them; "the barracks of an industry" the Hammonds called them. The goods-lines pass on embankments in and around, level with many of the bedroom windows, carrying the products of the men's work to South Africa, Nigeria,

Australia. The viaducts interweave with the railway lines and
30 with the canals below; the gasworks fit into a space
somewhere between them all, and the pubs and graceless
Methodist chapels stick up at intervals throughout. The green
stuff of the region forces its way where it can – and that is
almost everywhere – in stunted patches. Rough sooty grass
35 pushes through the cobbles; dock and nettle insist on a defiant
life in the rough and trampled earth-heaps at the corners of
the waste-pieces, undeterred by "dog-muck", cigarette
packets, old ashes; rank elder, dirty privet, and rosebay
willow-herb take hold on some of the "backs" or in the
40 walled-off space behind the Corporation Baths. All day and all
night the noises and smells of the district – factory hooters,
trains shunting, the stink of the gas-works – remind you that
life is a matter of shifts and clockings-in-and-out. The
children look improperly fed, inappropriately clothed, and as
45 though they could do with more sunlight and green fields.

But to the insider, these are small worlds, each as
homogeneous and well-defined as a village. Down below, on
the main road running straight into town, the bosses' cars
50 whirr away at five o'clock to converted farm-houses ten miles
out in the hills; the men stream up into their district. They
know it, as do all its inhabitants, in intimate detail –
automatically slipping up a snicket here or through a shared
lavatory block there; they know it as a group of tribal areas.
55 Pitt Street is certainly one of ours; just as certainly as Prince
Consort Street next to it is not, is over the boundary in
another parish. In my own part of Leeds I knew at ten years
old, as did all my contemporaries, both the relative status of
all the streets around us and where one part shaded into
60 another. Our gang fights were tribal fights, between streets or
groups of streets.

Similarly, one knows practically everybody, with an intimacy
of detail – that these people have a son who "got on" or
65 emigrated; that those have a daughter who went wrong or
one who married away and is doing well; that this old man
living alone on his pension shops at the horsemeat place in
town and smokes a sixpenny mixture of herbs; that this old
housewife is a fusspot and scours her window ledges and
70 steps twice a week, on her knees on a bit of old harding, and
even washes the brickwork up to shoulder height; that this
young woman had her black child after the annual visit of the

circus a few years ago; that this woman's idiot child can be trusted to run errands; that that old woman is always ready to sit up with an invalid for "a consideration"; that this man is a specially skilled worker and has been doing well for some time, so that he takes his family for a lavish week at Blackpool each summer and bought a television before anyone else; they have weekly booked seats at the Empire Theatre, the lad gets more ice-cream than any of his mates, and more than usually expensive presents at Christmas and birthdays.

1. Between what two different aspects of life does the author draw a distinction in the first paragraph?

2. Give in your own words, if necessary by referring to their contexts, the meaning of the following phrases:
   (a) 'these massed proletarian areas' (line 6),
   (b) 'a study in shades of dirty-grey' (line 10),
   (c) 'the barracks of an industry' (line 25),
   (d) 'a defiant life' (line 35),
   (e) 'the relative status of all the streets around us' (line 58).

3. (a) Why is 'the "better end"' (line 12) in inverted commas?
   (b) From the material in the second paragraph, deduce the various ways in which this area differs from the '·3"better end"'.
   About four statements are required.
   (c) What additional meaning is added by the author's use of the phrase 'to a visitor' in line 6?

4. In what sense is the name '"t' Moor"' evocative (line 19)?

5. How does the final sentence of paragraph 3 bring into focus the main ideas contained in that paragraph?

6. Why does the author introduce the references to the bosses' cars and houses in lines 49–50?

7. How does the author elaborate the idea of 'tribal areas' in lines 54–61?

8. What effect does the inclusion of the list of people in the fifth paragraph have on our view of life in this area?

9. Two ways of looking at this neighbourhood are expanded in this passage.
   (a) In a couple of sentences describe the main characteristics of these two viewpoints.
   (b) Say briefly why the author has provided this contrast of viewpoint.
10. What do you consider the advantages and disadvantages of being brought up in an area like this?

11. What additional meanings and feelings are given to the passage by the author's use of the following phrases:
   (a) 'gap-toothed' (line 17),
   (b) 'the green stuff of the region (lines 32–3),
   (c) 'dark and lowering canyons' (line 23)?

When you have completed your written answers to these questions, read on through the following commentary on the passage. You may find that it will help you to improve your answers before finally comparing them with the suggested answers on page 214.

The ideas that run through this passage are not really very complicated. Hoggart presents us with two different ways of looking at an area like this: the viewpoint of a person who visits such a neighbourhood, without knowing anything of the inner life of the inhabitants, is set against the view of the area held by the inhabitants, who are bound to have quite different feelings and associations for the place in which they carry on their working and social lives. The outsider, the visitor, sees the external appearance of the place. He notices its meanness, its squalor, its dirt, its poor buildings and the absence of parks and amenities. He notices the ever-present noise and smell of industry and, it is implied, he would contrast such living conditions with the cleanness and quiet of a middle-class housing estate. The 'insider', the person who has always lived in this area, experiences it from within and without judging it in these terms: he knows that a mere step outside his front door brings him into the vigorous and known life of the community.
The first short paragraph suggests the contrast between the private life going on within the home and the life of the community outside; this paragraph functions primarily as a connecting link with the previous section which had dealt with family life. It further suggests that stepping into the community life may be a pleasant experience. It may not be so bad to sit on the front

doorstep on a warm summer evening and chat to the neighbours and passers-by.

Having thus hinted that the local inhabitant would accept, easily and happily, his part in the life of the community, Hoggart elaborates, in the next two paragraphs, the view that an outsider or visitor might develop of the area. He conveys fully the unpleasant impressions that a visitor would inevitably carry away with him and produces, in a careful reader, a firm sense of the injustice that involves working people living in such conditions. The description is directed towards developing this sense of injustice in us; it is 'loaded' in the sense that the author employs words and phrases which do more than simply describe in an unemotional way. Many of the descriptive details have been chosen because they will evoke feelings in us.

In the second paragraph, the author is implying a contrast between this part of a town and the wealthier areas, where there would be light and air and brighter colours. He explains the poor condition of the houses by blaming the exploitation of landlords who will not spend money on property in which they themselves do not have to live, and from which they are assured of their rent anyway. Examples of the loaded phrases, to which I have referred, are 'gap-toothed' and 'dark and lowering canyons'. The former suggests a sad and ugly loss of physical beauty and the latter phrase describes the feeling that one might have of living in a pit, surrounded by the towering walls of factories, gas-works and the like, a hellish landscape. Hoggart quotes some other sociologists, the Hammonds, who have called the working men's houses 'the barracks of an industry'. The phrase neatly focuses an idea of the whole place being like an army camp with the inhabitants living constantly on the job, their entire lives governed by the demands of industry.

The third paragraph deals with the congestion and ugliness of the district and its lack of vegetation, of naturally growing plants and trees. Industrial buildings, railway lines, viaducts are packed close with houses, every available space being occupied with what contributes to the industry without regard for human well-being. Such vegetation as there is is so poor that Hoggart calls it 'the green stuff of the region' and, towards the end of this paragraph, he emphasises that even the sounds and smells of the area are a constant reminder of the routine of work. The last sentence of the third paragraph relates all that he has been saying to the appearance of the children. Of course, they could do with more sunlight and green fields: it is the absence of these things that he has been stressing throughout. That they are improperly fed and inappropriately clothed is an emphatic way of showing what has been implied: that the local people do not directly benefit from all this industrial activity, for the products are carried elsewhere – to 'South Africa, Nigeria, Australia' – and the profits line the pockets of the men who speed at five o'clock to their 'converted farm-houses ten miles out in the hills'.

Underlying this is a political attitude which includes an implied criticism of a society that exploits people by forcing them to live in unhealthy and unattractive environments. The author's sympathy for working-class people is present throughout and emerges clearly in the last two paragraphs of this extract. Despite their living conditions, the men here form closely-knit communities in which every detail of the area and almost everyone who lives in the locality are intimately known. The 'insider', the inhabitant, sees the area in a totally different way, not so much aware of it in general terms or contrasting it with other parts of the town, but knowing it as particular streets and individuals with their own unique histories. The bosses' cars carry them off to isolated homes where they are not part of a 'tribal area' and Hoggart introduces this detail, at this point in his description, because it contrasts so forcibly with the way the working men stream up into their own district, which is 'theirs' in a way that a district half a mile away is not.

The final paragraph of the extract is really a series of examples of the sort of people who could be found in a locality like this. They tend not to be the average people but to indicate the odd quirks of fate that affect lives or the noteworthy characteristics that make individuals identifiable. They are like brief case histories but they are not presented in a clinical, detached manner. Rather, this list suggests the varied and vigorous life of the community.

Down the mine

A point that might arise from what I have said about the passage from *The Uses of Literacy* is that although a deep concern for the lives and well-being of working people informs Richard Hoggart's description, he does not at any point create a simple, political issue in this extract. He describes a state of affairs and he analyses it, or he uses his description to illustrate distinctions and qualities about working class life that he wants us to recognise. At least at this stage in his book, he is more concerned to convey the **flavour** of life in an industrial community than he is to create an issue.

As a contrast, let us turn to a passage taken from George Orwell's essay 'Down the Mine'. He was also a writer who wished to make his readers more aware of the styles of living of the different levels of society and he also wished to convince his readers that they were morally bound to acknowledge the rights and the work of other people on whom they depended for maintaining much of the comfort of civilised life. Perhaps because this extract comes from a relatively short essay, the main point, the idea, emerges very clearly. It is a fine example of descriptive writing being obviously used in the service of ideas. Everything that Orwell describes in this essay contributes to one general point, which is convincingly stated towards the end of the essay.

Orwell invites us to share in his experience of visiting a coal mine, to accompany someone who, as he says, could no more be a coal-miner than 'perform on a flying trapeze' or 'win the Grand National'. The first part of the following passage is extracted from the early portion of the essay and is a good example of descriptive writing designed to involve the reader in the imaginative exploration of a situation. But, as I have said, Orwell does not offer imaginative description alone: he proceeds to elaborate strong views on the relationships between different parts of society. I have, therefore, taken a further extract, from towards the end of the essay, which constitutes a powerful plea for the reader to recognise the vital importance of the job of coal-mining. This essay was written in 1937, when coal production was at its height in this country and when coal was the major source of energy.

Read through the passage several times and then answer in writing the questions that follow it. You will find suggested answers on page 215. However, before you consult the model answers, read the commentary that follows the questions and try to improve your own answers.

What is surprising, on the other hand, is the immense horizontal distances that have to be travelled underground

Before I had been down a mine I had vaguely imagined the miner stepping out of the cage and getting to work on a ledge of coal a few yards away. I had not realised that before he even gets to his work he may have had to creep along passages as long as from London Bridge to Oxford Circus. In the beginning, of course, a mine shaft is sunk somewhere near a seam of coal. But as that seam is worked out and fresh seams are followed up, the workings get further and further from the pit bottom. If it is a mile from the pit bottom to the coal face, that is probably an average distance; three miles is a fairly normal one; there are even said to be a few mines where it is as much as five miles. But these distances bear no relation to distances above ground. For in all that mile or three miles as it may be, there is hardly anywhere outside the main road, and not many places even there, where a man can stand upright.

You do not notice the effect of this till you have gone a few hundred yards. You start off, stooping slightly, down the dim-lit gallery, eight or ten feet wide and about five high, with the walls built up with slabs of shale, like the stone walls in Derbyshire. Every yard or two there are wooden props holding up the beams and girders; some of the girders have buckled into fantastic curves under which you have to duck. Usually it is bad-going underfoot – thick dust or jagged chunks of shale, and in some mines where there is water it is as mucky as a farmyard. Also there is the track for the coal tubs, like a miniature railway track with sleepers a foot or two apart, which is tiresome to walk on. Everything is grey with shale dust; there is a dusty fiery smell which seems to be the same in all mines. You see mysterious machines of which you never learn the purpose, and bundles of tools slung together on wires, and sometimes mice darting away from the beam of the lamps. They are surprisingly common, especially in mines where there are or have been horses. It would be interesting to know how they got there in the first place; possibly by falling down the shaft – for they say a mouse can fall any distance uninjured, owing to its surface area being so large relative to its weight. You press yourself against the wall to make way for lines of tubs jolting slowly towards the shaft, drawn by an endless steel cable operated from the surface. You creep through sacking curtains and thick wooden doors which, when they are opened, let out fierce blasts of air. These doors are an important part of the ventilation system. The exhausted air is sucked out of one shaft by means of fans, and the fresh air enters the other of its own accord. But if left to itself the air will take the shortest way round, leaving the deeper workings unventilated; so all the short cuts have to be

50 partitioned off.

At the start, to walk stooping is rather a joke, but it is a joke that soon wears off. I am handicapped by being exceptionally tall, but when the roof falls to four feet or less it is a tough job

55 for anybody except a dwarf or a child. You not only have to bend double, you have also got to keep your head up all the while so as to see the beams and girders and dodge them when they come. You have, therefore, a constant crick in the neck, but this is nothing to the pain in your knees and thighs.

60 After half a mile it becomes (I am not exaggerating) an unbearable agony. You begin to wonder whether you will ever get to the end – still more, how on earth you are going to get back. Your pace grows slower and slower. You come to a stretch of a couple of hundred yards where it is all

65 exceptionally low and you have to work yourself along in a squatting position. Then suddenly the roof opens out to a mysterious height – scene of an old fall of rock, probably – and for twenty whole yards you can stand upright. The relief is overwhelming. But after this there is another low stretch of

70 a hundred yards and then a succession of beams which you have to crawl under. You go down on all fours; even this is a relief after the squatting business. But when you come to the end of the beams and try to get up again, you find that your knees have temporarily struck work and refuse to lift you.

75 You call a halt, ignominiously, and say that you would like to rest for a minute or two. Your guide (a miner) is sympathetic. He knows that your muscles are not the same as his. "Only another four hundred yards," he says encouragingly; you feel that he might as well say another four hundred miles. But

80 finally you do somehow creep as far as the coal face. You have gone a mile and taken the best part of an hour; a miner would do it in not much more than twenty minutes. Having got there, you have to sprawl in the coal dust and get your strength back for several minutes before you can even watch

85 the work in progress with any kind of intelligence . . .

Watching coal-miners at work, you realise momentarily what different universes people inhabit. Down there where coal is dug is a sort of world apart which one can quite easily go

90 through life without ever hearing about. Probably a majority

of people would even prefer not to hear about it. Yet it is the
absolutely necessary counterpart of our world above. Practically everything we do, from eating an ice to crossing the
Atlantic, and from baking a loaf to writing a novel, involves
95 the use of coal, directly or indirectly. For all the arts of peace
coal is needed; if war breaks out it is needed all the more. In
time of revolution the miner must go on working or the
revolution must stop, for revolution as much as reaction
needs coal. Whatever may be happening on the surface, the
100 hacking and shovelling have got to continue without a pause,
or at any rate without pausing for more than a few weeks at
the most . . . But on the whole we are not aware of it; we all
know that we "must have coal", but we seldom or never
remember what coal-getting involves. Here am I sitting
105 writing in front of my comfortable coal fire. It is April but I
still need a fire. Once a fortnight the coal cart drives up to the
door and men in leather jerkins carry the coal indoors in stout
sacks smelling of tar and shoot it clanking into the coal-hole
under the stairs. It is only very rarely, when I make a definite
110 mental effort, that I connect this coal with that far-off labour
in the mines. It is just "coal" – something that I have got to
have; black stuff that arrives mysteriously from nowhere in
particular, like manna except that you have to pay for it. You
could quite easily drive a car right across the north of England
115 and never once remember that hundreds of feet below the
road you are on the miners are hacking at the coal. Yet in a
sense it is the miners who are driving your car forward. Their
lamp-lit world down there is as necessary to the daylight
world above as the root is to the flower.

1. What means does Orwell use in the first paragraph to
   emphasise the distance that a miner has to travel underground?

2. Consider the point behind the description in the second
   paragraph and then write down a statement from the first
   paragraph which best summarises this point.

3. Write a short paragraph summarising the conditions which
   make it difficult to walk along the mine passages.

4. Why does the author continually refer to 'you' in the second
   and third paragraphs?

5. What meaning is added by the use of the word 'ignominiously'
   in line 75?

6. Explain the realisation summed up in the phrase 'what different universes people inhabit' (lines 87–8).

7. 'Probably a majority of people would even prefer not to hear about it.' (lines 90–1)
   Why do you think Orwell includes this sentence?

8. Look through the passage and consider Orwell's references to himself.
   (a) What impression of himself does he wish to convey to the reader?
   (b) Why do you think he wishes to convey this impression?

9. In the last paragraph, by what means does Orwell:
   (a) demonstrate the idea that every aspect of life depends on coal and
   (b) demonstrate the idea that the ordinary man does not usually appreciate this fact.

The fact that I have asked few questions about individual words and phrases is a reflection of the straightforwardness of this passage; Orwell is writing for the average man and aiming to present his ideas in as clear a manner as possible. There is nothing that is really obscure in what he says. However, the *way* in which he presents his ideas, the strategy that he employs to convince his reader, is worthy of a closer examination and brief commentary. In order to answer questions 1, 4, 7, 8 and 9 above, an awareness of Orwell's strategy is helpful.

Orwell uses a considerable variety of types of statement in the course of this extract. Occasionally, he is simply explaining, for example, the purpose of the heavy wooden doors in the mine passages, or the reasons why there tends to be a great distance between the shaft and the coal face. This explanation is, however, incidental to his primary intention in writing. Similarly, the speculations, for example, about the presence of mice in coal mines or the sudden alterations in roof-height, are not central to his purposes. Taken as a whole, this is not a technical or even a layman's account of mining processes and his purposes are certainly not primarily informative.

At times, Orwell makes statements that are apparently personal. He refers to himself, to his wrong impression that miners would step out of the cage and start work on a ledge a few yards away or to his failure to connect the coal in his home fire with the mining activities that go on underground. Yet these personal statements are obviously incidental also to his primary purpose: he is not concerned with his own thoughts and feelings in the way that we noted Edwin Muir to be. In no serious sense does he focus our attention on his personality.

His descriptive passages might, for a moment, be compared with the description in the extract from Laurie Lee's book. Orwell's description of the mine is clear and unadorned, not elaborate and full of associations like Lee's description of his Spanish journey. He is obviously not inviting us into an imaginative experience for its own sake: Orwell is not primarily out to entertain us.

If he is not out to entertain us, it is also true that he is not concerned to provoke us into thinking in a complex way. We do not here have to appreciate different points of view as we do when reading the passage from Richard Hoggart's book.

Many of Orwell's strategies, the ways in which he presents his ideas, arise from the simple fact that his basic aim might not be readily acceptable to the reader. In the end, he is virtually telling us that we are selfish and unaware, that we have never taken the trouble to appreciate the hardships of the miner's job and that we enjoy the luxuries of life in a thoughtless, self-indulgent manner. Naturally, this 'attack' on his reader is not openly stated as such; it emerges by implication. The problem for a writer of Orwell's convictions, who is aiming to produce a change of attitude in his reader, is how to 'get at' the reader, how to convince him, without actually annoying him to the extent that he will put the book down.

He solves this problem in a number of skilful ways. He introduces himself into his essay, making himself appear as the average, unthinking man, almost an excessively simple man, one who had not even realised that mines stretched for vast distances underground. So, he makes himself an amiable companion for the ordinary reader and avoids giving the impression that he has all the answers and the reader is morally bound to listen. He also very effectively invites us to share in the discomforts he experienced in visiting a mine. In imagination, our muscles too must be aching by the end of the third paragraph and so, we can hardly deny the justice of his view that we should be aware of what other people have to endure in their working conditions for the general benefit of society. Furthermore, he implies throughout that, even though, like him, we have not thought about all this before, we are unlikely to be amongst the majority that 'would even prefer not to hear about it.' Finally, he illustrates his point about our dependence on coal with a number of examples and, at the end of this passage, he neatly demonstrates the unawareness of most people by introducing the simple, ordinary experience of driving a car across the north of England.

I would wish to emphasise that this passage is not journalistic propaganda. The propagandist aims to manipulate his reader into closing his eyes to all other possible points of view and to swallow wholesale the author's beliefs or doctrines. When we read Orwell's work, we genuinely extend our awareness without the author having to unreasonably manipulate feelings such as guilt, sentimentality or prejudice in order to force us into agreement with him. Yet, the primary intention of this writer is to make us see things from his point of view: this passage is a fine example of descriptive and explanatory writing used entirely in the service of an overriding conviction.

Summary of key points and rules in chapter 3

1. Develop the capacity for perceiving the intentions of the author. It is vital to understand what his aims are if you are to answer comprehension questions fully and intelligently.

2. Writers of non-fiction books, which describe and explain the real world around them as they see it, usually aim to extend the reader's appreciation of things. In approaching a descriptive passage for comprehension, distinguish what the writer is offering you: is it an insight into himself, a new imaginative experience, the opportunity to think, or an invitation to develop a fresh attitude to something?

3. Unless you have a general sense of the writer's intentions, you will not be able to pay attention to details and to answer precise questions without a disturbing feeling that the passage as a whole does not mean anything to you.

Chapter 4
Understanding Arguments, Opinions and Explanations

Attending to ideas

In the last chapter, we were primarily concerned with passages of writing which was essentially descriptive, although the last few extracts in that chapter also included explanatory and, in the case of Orwell, argumentative writing. Those writers were, above all, attempting to convey to us the quality of an experience, sometimes for its own sake, as in the description of the Spanish village by Laurie Lee, and sometimes in order to jolt us into an awareness which might cause a change in our political or social attitudes. Generally speaking, those writers were more concerned to offer the reader an extension of experience through imagination than to present him with a range of ideas. We shall now move on to consider some passages in which description, if it is present at all, is far less important and where the primary emphasis is on the arguments and ideas of the author. The extracts in this chapter require of the reader not so much a readiness to allow his imagination to be extended as an ability to understand abstract language and notions.

When you read books or articles which deal primarily with ideas and arguments, a particular sort of attention is required from you. Instead of recreating imaginatively the places and people about which a descriptive author writes, exercising your senses of seeing, hearing, smelling etc. in imagination, so that you can respond precisely to the human or natural situation which the descriptive writing suggests, you have to concentrate, in the case of a passage of abstract thought, on the main lines of the argument. This involves perceiving the various points that the author is making, retaining the main ideas clearly in your mind, and noticing the ways in which the various points are developed and related to one another. The type of attention required of the reader is not so much imaginative as thoughtful; what he must work towards is a clear grasp of the stages by which the argument develops, an appreciation of the author's processes of thought.

All this sounds very demanding and difficult and it is of course true that, at times, abstract thinking may be the most painful demand that can be made upon us. But, take courage — you already spend quite a lot of time thinking in abstractions. Consider some of the other subjects you study. In history, you may be faced with a mass of details, facts and ideas about a particular period of time or sequence of events and, with the aid of teachers and books, must work towards perceiving an order in them: discovering, for example, that one major treaty had various results on the economies of the countries that had signed it; or that there was a connection between the foreign policy of a particular prime minister and the nature of the support upon which he depended in his country. In geography, for example, you might look carefully at various glaciated areas, identifying the distinctive land-forms of the areas and discovering that certain land-forms are common to all such areas. You may then have to proceed to explain how they have come to be produced in this way.

There are basically two processes at work in thought of this sort, in abstract thinking about any subject or situation. We break down the mass of material and facts into smaller details and aspects, identifying, within the overall subject, the various elements that constitute the matter we are studying. This is the first process. The second involves us in making general statements about these points or aspects of the subject which bring out what they have in common and which help us see them in a more coherent pattern. This effort to make general statements about the subject may involve sorting the details, facts or ideas, into categories and also perceiving cause and effect amongst the material we are working with. For example, once we have identified the various events in a given historical period, we may be able to see how some situations caused others to occur.

These two processes of breaking something down into its components and then putting these components together in such a way that they make sense to us are the two essential processes in any kind of thinking. They can be called **analysis** and **synthesis**. In practice, of course, it is unlikely that the two processes of thought would be pursued independently; more often we would be working away at analysing the main elements in a subject of study and synthesising them into generalisations at the same time.

Analysis and synthesis proceed together and it is frequently difficult to separate them out but, in thinking about a subject, it is likely that we would proceed in the following manner. When we

70

approach a body of facts, we probably have a rough idea of the sort of generalisation or synthesis which would enable us to put them into perspective and create an orderly interpretation, and we would then begin to analyse the facts, to examine each in turn, with the general interpretation or synthesis in mind. If each fact falls neatly into place within the overall interpretation, then we will not need to alter the generalisation we had anticipated at the start but, what is more likely, if we are thinking at all originally, is that various facts will assume a greater importance than we had at first expected and that, as we look at the material more carefully, we will gradually modify our original idea. The final generalisation or synthesis is likely to be different from the guess we had made before proceeding with close scrutiny of the available facts. We may even have to completely abandon the original possible interpretation and start again, perhaps many times.

What I have just been briefly describing is the process of exploratory thinking but when someone is in a position to write a book or article on some subject, the exploratory thought might reasonably be expected to have already taken place. The author, before he writes his book, will have already worked over his subject, examined the details and decided upon the major generalisations that he wishes to make. A good writer will have brought order into the mass of material and will present a clear sequence of generalisations, each of which is elaborated or supported by detailed evidence.

Our main concern, in approaching a piece of writing which is composed of arguments and explanations, must be to develop the skill of speedily identifying the main sequence of ideas, those ideas which together make up what I defined as the synthesis of the subject under consideration. These are the generalisations and interpretations which the writer has toiled towards formulating before he has written his book. If you do not make an adequate effort to grasp the main threads of the argument, it is almost certain that you will become hopelessly preoccupied with minor details which the author is using merely to support his argument or as a context in which to set his main generalising statements. This development of your ability to go to the heart of an argument is important not only for the GCE O-level examination but also if you are to be able, in the future, to cope with the massive quantity of print that floods before us in this age. We need to be capable of reading swiftly, absorbing what is essential and dwelling on the more minor aspects of the argument only when they have some particular importance or interest for us.

Identifying the main idea

Let us start by considering the opening paragraph to a chapter from a history book called *The Age of Improvement*, by Asa Briggs. The chapter is sub-titled 'England and the French Revolution'. Read through the paragraph carefully and identify the central point that the author is making. This is not quite as simple an exercise as may first appear, for the author approaches his central point obliquely, not stating it at once but allowing it to arise out of a background of other ideas, a setting which involves stating and dismissing a possible alternative view of the period he is about to discuss.

Few societies have been more secure in the belief that they can control their own destinies than the English, particularly the self-confident society of the late eighteenth century. Although the American Revolution had divided and embit-
5 tered English politicians and created domestic situations of acute tension, and the industrial revolution was posing problems which were to generate new bitterness, the course of events between 1783 and 1789 suggested that the years of crisis were being forgotten. "The varied and accumulated
10 misfortunes which for a long series of years oppressed, and had almost overwhelmed the commonwealth, were already erased from the recollection. A mild and happy calm had smoothed these troubled waves." There was bitterness in the rivalry between Pitt and Fox and signs of dispute and conflict
15 in politics outside Westminster, but it seemed as if the consequences of these internal differences would be settled by Englishmen in their own way. Instead, events outside England, the French Revolution and its Napoleonic aftermath, dictated much of what happened inside England in the
20 long period from 1789 to 1815. The way into the nineteenth century led across the battlefield as well as through the cotton mill and the iron foundry. As the Whig lawyer, Cockburn, remarked, "everything was connected with the Revolution in France, which for twenty years was, or was made, all in all,
25 everything; not this thing or that thing, but literally everything was soaked in this one event."

Make sure that you can identify the **main** idea in this paragraph and can explain how it is introduced and emphasised before you go on to read the following paragraphs.

Briggs starts by making a very general comment about the English, stating that, as a nation, they always believe that they can control their own destiny and determine their own future and that this self-confident belief in independent control of the nation's rection was particularly evident in the years that led up to 1789. He quotes from a contemporary source to show that Englishmen felt, at that time, optimistic and that they would be able to sort out their internal difficulties — which he merely notes in passing — in their own way.

This, then, is a brief, generalised view of the period he is about to discuss, and the author starts in this way partly in order to give the reader a glimpse of the tenor of life, the general attitude at the time, and partly in order to provide a contrast to the main idea in the paragraph, which he proceeds to state. This main idea is 'events outside England ... dictated much of what happened inside England in the long period from 1789 to 1815.' The last two sentences in the paragraph restate and briefly explore this main idea: England was forced to look outwards and become involved in the Napoleonic wars and was, therefore, not allowed to concentrate solely on her internal industrial growth, and the French Revolution made an enormous impact on English thought and action to the extent that everything seemed to be intimately connected with it.

It is worth standing back from the actual material in the paragraph I have quoted and looking at the structure of the thought because it is an example of a very common method of presenting an argument. The author here considers one possible interpretation of his material and rejects it by stating what he considers to be the correct interpretation. In this particular paragraph, it is, of course, simply a matter of placing contemporary expectations of the likely course of events against a historian's view of what actually happened but this procedure is similar to the writer who has examined material that has hitherto been interpreted in one way and discovers that he disagrees with that commonly held interpretation. When he comes to write his own book or article, he may well present the widely held view and then, by examining the evidence afresh, demolish it in favour of his own interpretation.

Just such a procedure is followed by the authors of an article published in *New Society* in May 1975. It is titled 'How Far from the Madding Crowd?' and it examines the effects that living in crowded circumstances in cities may have upon people. The purpose of the article is to demolish the theory that crowding itself produces social problems and psychological abnormalities. It shows how this theory has been developed from experiments involving the crowding of animals together and then the observation of their behaviour but it points out that there is no true comparison between the behaviour of rats crowded together in cages and the behaviour of humans crowded in cities. The authors — Claude S. Fischer and Mark Baldassare — provide evidence which contradicts the theory that animal-behaviour patterns are also present in humans. Having done that, they proceed to re-examine the nature of city life and the evidence that urban crowding itself produces the problems and strains associated with living in cities. The passage I shall quote comes from this second section of the rticle and it is followed by a further extract from towards the end of the article in which the authors present their own theory of the causes of urban problems.

This is a difficult article and it will require careful reading and close attention to my introductory paragraph above. Before you start reading it, I ought to mention that the word 'ethology' means 'the studying of behaviour patterns'. 'Animal ethologists' are scientists concerned with patterns of animal behaviour.

Are crowding theories applicable to cities? Urban critics too often make the leap from rat cages to cities.

5 First, city dwellers live in private, separated dwellings (houses and flats) and not in public territories. Thus, they live at *many* densities, not just one. The facts also indicate that there is less overcrowding in urban dwelling units than in rural ones. It is of course true that urban people find themselves in crowds more often than others, but how often,
10 and to what effect is unclear. Unlike caged rats, people can
·   'escape' intolerable densities. For example, the urbanite who dislikes crowded trains can drive to work; or the individual who cannot tolerate the density of people in his neighbourhood can take a walk in the park.
15
Several investigations of the association between dense

neighbourhoods and pathological behaviour have provided disappointing evidence for the proposition that crowding produces abnormal behaviour. An association between
20 density *per se* (persons per square mile) and pathology (mortality, mental hospital admissions, delinquency) does exist, but it is largely because persons prone to such behaviour have little economic or social choice but to live in low-income, high-density areas...
·25

Does crowding cause urban violence? This, on the surface at least, seems to be one point where the urban critics score. Substantial increases in the rates of violence take place as cities enlarge, particularly in America. Homicide rates in the
30 cities with over a million population run three times greater than those in rural areas, while aggravated assaults run five times greater. It is tempting, then, to explain these statistics as aggressive reactions to crowding. However, such an explanation runs into serious contradictions and anomalies.
·35

The idea faces an immediate difficulty when one considers historical trends and cultural differences in aggression. While violent crimes have been increasing in urban areas over the past few decades, the world's industrial cities have been
40 *declining* in density for over 70 years. Cities with massive densities, such as Tokyo and Hong Kong, have violent crime rates which are fractions of those in small American cities. Also 'crowding' (or density) and city size are hardly the same variables and cannot be used interchangeably. Recent studies
45 by S. J. Webb have shown that while the population size of a city correlates with the violent crime rate, the density of a city does not.

Some final reflections on incidents of violence should
50 hammer nails into this argument's coffin. Despite what the ethologists have led us to believe, violent crime most often occurs indoors and between inmates. Thus there is little support for the idea that aggression occurs between 'territory-invading' males, or in overcrowded urban situations. Even
55 when violence takes place against strangers, it usually occurs out of public view...

Yet, of course, urban problems *do* exist. There is city crime, whether violent or not, for example. And sometimes for
60 better, sometimes for worse, there is a wide range of 'deviant'

behaviour in cities: vice, avant-garde life styles, group conflict, political dissent. However, we believe that the explanation is *not* to be found in the psychology of crowding, but in changes in social structure which occur with increases
65 in community size. Briefly, our argument is that increasing population makes it more possible for groups of unusual, non-typical individuals to become sufficient in number to support strong and viable sub-cultures. The types of group are diverse — ethnic, religious, chess lovers, intellectuals,
70 criminals. For each of these, increasing numbers bring friends, resources, organisations, supportive services, meeting places and power.

Take urban violence as an example. In the United States, this
75 seems to be due to the disproportionate presence and concentration in large cities of certain regional and ethnic groups which carry with them "sub-cultures of violence". In addition, cities in general produce criminal and crime-prone sub-cultures simply because there are more criminal targets
80 (stores, wealth, affluent residents). Lastly, the presence of criminals themselves in large numbers — whether crowded or not — generates criminal sub-cultures. These sub-cultures are prone to violence, against others and themselves. Thus, cities can produce crime, but not because of overcrowding.
85
It is sub-culture, nurtured by the size of population in cities, which produces much of the strife and deviance associated with urban life. However, this very same process also produces many of the benefits of urban life: artistic, cultural
90 and intellectual activity, differing life styles, innumerable economic and social opportunities, and sufficient services to cater to all needs. If this is so, then we must live with the irony that the blessings of urban life perhaps cannot be achieved without also accepting some of its curses.

This is by no means an easy passage, as I have already said, and you are almost bound to have experienced some difficulty with the authors' language, which constantly tends towards the abstract and the use of words which would be familiar to other students of sociology but may not be so familiar to the rest of us. However, let me emphasise again that the most important thing in dealing with any piece of abstract writing, is to go straight to the main ideas, to the central line of argument running through the writing and then, having grasped that, to let the more detailed arguments and distinctions fall into place.

Remember two of the points that I have made about this passage:
1. the authors are arguing against the view that crowding, or high-density living, itself produces abnormal behaviour and social problems;
2. the authors have already dismissed, to their own satisfaction, the evidence previously used to support the view that crowding causes the problems of city life.

Read the passage again and answer the following questions in writing. They have been designed to help you concentrate on the main argument of this extract. Suggested answers may be found on page 216.

1. (a) In the paragraph that begins on line 4, the authors elaborate the main difference between the conditions of crowding for city dwellers and the conditions of crowding for rats put into cages for experimental purposes. Quote the shortest statement in that paragraph of this main difference.
(b) In the same paragraph, the authors elaborate this essential difference between experimentally caged rats and urbanites by making a comparison between living conditions in cities and living conditions in rural areas. What point emerges from this comparison?
(c) The authors also expand the main idea of this paragraph by restating the idea in more precise terms and supporting that restatement with two examples. Put this restatement into your own words and show how the two examples support it.

2. The paragraph that begins on line 16 suggests that the relationship that has been observed between crowding (density) and abnormal behaviour (pathology) is not simply the result of crowding itself. What reason do the authors state for the presence of pathological behaviour in densely populated parts of cities?

3. Why is it tempting to assume that crowding causes violence (see lines 26–34)?

4. (a) For what purpose do the authors compare Tokyo and Hong Kong with small American cities in the paragraph beginning on line 36?

(b) Put the idea in the final sentence of this paragraph into your own words.

5. In the paragraph beginning on line 49, the authors are opposing an interpretation of the nature of violence in cities which has been put forward as a result of observing animal behaviour in confined, crowded circumstances.
(a) What do you suppose this interpretation by animal ethologists to be?
(b) Quote a statement from this paragraph that effectively demolishes the argument based on animal behaviour.

6. The last three paragraphs present the authors' view of what causes urban problems of crime and 'deviant' behaviour. Briefly summarise their view and show how it differs from the argument they are opposing.

The imaginary objector

The passage we have just looked at is primarily an academic exercise though it does have some important implications for commonly-held attitudes towards a range of real and important human situations; for example, the authors refer elsewhere in their article to a misguided American publication, which argues against the desirability of different races mixing freely in cities on the grounds that crowding together different animal species leads to conflict. This sort of argument could disastrously influence more humane policies on racial integration. Nevertheless, although the article I have quoted from is primarily a sociological investigation written for intellectuals, the method whereby the argument proceeds is one which is used in many different types of writing.

Using someone else's inadequate argument or wrong-headed opinions as a starting point for discussion is a very useful ploy. It provides a point of departure from which the author's own argument can develop and it can yield a contrast which points the writer's opinions all the more clearly. By referring back at intervals to the opposing viewpoint, the author may be able to convey more clearly the distinctive nature of his own argument. It is worth your while thinking carefully about this way of presenting ideas: not only will this help you to cope with similar passages for comprehension in the exam, it will enable you to tighten up your own opinionative and argumentative writing, but more of that in chapter 10.

Let us move on to a passage which works by extending and developing this method of presenting ideas or opinions through opposing a different set of ideas. In this passage, the author makes use of an imaginary objector, someone who is going to be difficult to convince of the validity of the author's beliefs. In the course of the passage he carries on an imaginary argument with this objector and is thereby able to dramatise the argument. The reader will either hold the writer's view of the subject and consequently feel at one with his attitudes and correspondingly pleased at the demolition of the imaginary objector, or he will hold the objector's views and either be forced reluctantly to agree with the writer or to find some way of arguing back.

This passage is taken from an article by Christopher Wood in a book called *Common Sense about Smoking*. Read it through several times and answer the questions that follow but, before checking with the suggested answers on page 217, consider the points made in the commentary after the questions and see if you can improve your answers.

It is often said, "I know all about the risk to my health, but I think that the risk is worth it." When this statement is true it should be accepted. Everyone has a right to choose what risks he takes, however great they may be. However, often the
5   statement really means, "I have a nasty feeling that smoking is bad for my health, but I would rather not think about it." With some of these people the bluff can be called and they can be asked to explain what they think the risk to their own health is. When this is done few get very far in personal terms.
10   The bare fact that 23,000 people died of lung cancer last year in Great Britain often fails to impress an individual. When it is explained that this is the equivalent of one every twenty-five minutes or is four times as many as those killed on the roads, the significance is more apparent. The one-in-eight risk of
15   dying of lung cancer for the man who smokes twenty-five or more cigarettes a day may be better appreciated if an analogy is used. If, when you boarded a plane, the girl at the top of the steps were to welcome you aboard with the greeting, "I am pleased that you are coming with us – only one in eight of our
20   planes crashes," how many would think again and make other arrangements? Alternatively, the analogy of Russian Roulette may appeal. The man smoking twenty-five or more a day runs the same risks between the ages of thirty and sixty

as another who buys a revolver with 250 chambers and inserts one live bullet and on each of his birthdays spins the chamber, points the revolver at his head, and pulls the trigger. One of the difficulties in impressing these facts on people is that, despite the current epidemic of lung cancer, because it is a disease which kills relatively quickly, there are many who have as yet no experience of it among their family or friends.

This contrasts with the picture of chronic bronchitis, a knowledge of which is common to most people because it is a long-drawn-out disease and death usually only follows many years of suffering. However, most smokers reserve the term chronic bronchitis for elderly people with severe breathlessness. They fail to appreciate that this is only the last stage of a disease which probably began twenty years ago with a chronic productive morning cough which they may themselves have, but which they prefer to call by the euphemism of "smoker's cough".

The readiness with which people will suggest an association between disease and air pollution by chimney smoke or by diesel fumes provides an interesting contrast to their reluctance to accept the relation to cigarette smoking. One of the important differences between the two being that "they" ought to do something about air pollution, while "I" would have to change smoking habits. That those living in cities have a greater liability to lung cancer and bronchitis is true, but the difference between town and country is considerably less than the difference between smoking and not smoking. It is also likely that town smoke and cigarette smoke are cumulative in their effects. It therefore follows that if one is exposed to the danger of living in a town it is all the more important to refrain from augmenting the risk by smoking. While there is no doubt that the black, stinking fumes from a poorly maintained diesel lorry are most unpleasant, there is as yet no evidence of any direct harm. Mechanics in garages and London traffic policemen, who might be expected to show an effect if there is one, do not appear to have any excess of lung cancer.

Describing the part played by smoking in these diseases, or in any other such as coronary artery disease, tuberculosis, rupture or duodenal ulcer, in personal terms which could be appreciated by and would be particularly relevant to the

individual concerned, would not be justifiable unless a
remedy was available. There is, in fact, ample evidence to
70 refute the commonly held view, "Well – it is too late for me to
do anything about it." The facts show that the risk of
developing lung cancer decreases strikingly in those who stop
smoking in comparison with those who continue. The
improvement in symptoms in bronchitis is often striking, and
75 in some early cases it is probable that permanent cure
follows.

1. (a) What sentence in the first paragraph most clearly shows that
   the author wishes to present himself as utterly fair and
   reasonable?
   (b) Where else in the extract does he present himself as humane
   and reasonable?

2. What does the author suggest is a characteristic attitude of the
   people he wishes to oppose (see lines 1–9)?

3. What is the main point the author wishes to impress on heavy
   smokers in the first paragraph? What method of argument does
   he use in order to reinforce this point?

4. In the first paragraph, the author implies two reasons why
   smokers do not take the risk of lung cancer seriously. What are
   those two reasons?

5. How, according to the author, do heavy smokers avoid facing
   up to the risk of chronic bronchitis (lines 32–40)?

6. For what reason do you think the author comments on the
   'association between disease and air pollution' in the third
   paragraph?

This passage proceeds by, first of all, defining the attitude that the
author believes characterises the heavy smoker who does not
wish to abandon his smoking habit. Wood's opening is quite
skilful: he quotes the sort of statement that his imaginary objector
might very well make and then he uses this statement in two
ways. To begin with, it gives him an opportunity to show how
reasonable he is about the whole issue ("Everyone has the right
to choose what risks they take . . .") and so to commend himself

to the reader as an entirely trustworthy and fair judge in this matter of smoking. Conceding a point to the opposition is a useful ploy which creates a favourable impression of impartiality and invites confidence. Secondly, he is able to demonstrate that the smoker's statement cannot often be taken at face value; he suggests that the smoker asserts that he knows all about the risk merely in order to fend off further attack, that the heavy smoker defends himself from realising his danger by not thinking about it in personal terms. This, of course, gives the author an opportunity to write as if he were forcing some heavily smoking objector to face up to facts and, in the rest of this first paragraph, he takes the statistics for lung-cancer deaths and the proportion of heavy smokers who succumb to the disease and drives home the significance of these figures by means of analogy or situations of comparable danger.

The method of argument, or of presentation of a viewpoint, in the first paragraph is not working essentially by logic and rational argument. The author is not appealing to the intellect of his readers so much as to their feelings. He attempts to stir what must be feelings mainly of guilt and fear in his imaginary objectors. The person who does not smoke or has abandoned the habit will nod in easy agreement and relief that he need not take too much notice of all this danger but the heavy smoker is bound, if he responds to the article at all, to feel some undercurrents of fear. He has quite possibly not thought about the danger in personal terms nor had to confront the horror of a member of his family or one of his friends dying of cancer.

Smokers may not take seriously the lung cancer risk for either of those two reasons and the author moves remorselessly on to show, in his second paragraph, how smokers avoid facing up to the danger of bronchitis by calling it 'smoker's cough' and pretending that the disease is caused by old age rather than by a life-long ill-treatment of the lungs.

By this stage, the reader will have realised that the author is virtually listing the attitudes and comments that smokers often produce in defence of their habit and then showing how these attitudes are false. He is undermining the position of his imaginary objector by showing how his every move is a defensive one. The author probes the smoker's real feelings and motives for producing such defences. So, the whole of the third paragraph is not strictly relevant to the case against heavy smoking: it is there in order to demonstrate and demolish the defensive arguments of the smoker-under-attack. The latter, the author suggests, would be likely in such a conversation to say, 'There's no point in worrying about the effects of smoking when the atmosphere is so polluted anyway.' The author effectively cuts off this particular escape from facing up to the issue.

Finally, in this extract, the author reasserts himself as a man of humane and reasonable disposition who is by no means attacking other people for the pleasure of feeling his own strength. He slips in yet another of the smoker's characteristic defences – 'It's too late for me to do anything about it' – and states that there is evidence to show that stopping smoking will reduce the risk of contracting cancer and will alleviate bronchitic conditions even if the smoker has been puffing away happily for decades. He, therefore, presents himself as concerned about cure and human well-being rather than the effective demolition of other people's defensive attitudes and resistance to change.

It is clear that this sort of writing is more closely allied to the parson's sermon and the politician's speech than it is to the primarily logical argument and production of evidence giving rise to theories which we noted in the previous extract from the article on city life. That is not to say that it does not contain entirely acceptable ideas, logically developed, but what I *am* saying is that this author is more interested in touching the feelings of his readers than he is in interesting us in new theories. He wants to cause a change of attitude in his imaginary objector which will lead to a change in habits and so, as well as confronting the objector with the whole truth, he must present himself as trustworthy. In much the same way, a politician may attempt to encourage confidence and win new supporters by assuming a reasonable or forceful manner and may even demonstrate his fairmindedness by conceding the occasional point to the opposition.

In achieving these aims, Christopher Wood's use of the imaginary objector is very important. It enables him to dramatise and focus his argument without annoying the reader as much as he would if he had attacked him directly. He is able to produce quite powerful criticisms of the 'double-think', the wilful blindness of the heavy smoker, without pointing his finger straight at the heavily-smoking reader. Furthermore, the type of statement that the objector might make becomes, whenever such a statement is introduced into the article, a starting-point for a further attack on his foolishness. And so, the shadowy presence of the imaginary objector enables this author to develop, expand and emphasise his case.

Accepting the author's insight

So far in this chapter, I have been stressing the need for you to develop the capacity for grasping the main lines of thought in certain passages, for following the growth of the central argument whilst distinguishing those main points from what is just evidence in support of the argument or elaboration of the main points. We have also looked at ways in which argumentative writing may be given coherence and order by opposing some viewpoint, the writer bringing forward evidence to support an alternative interpretation. In the last extract that we considered, the author did not so much bring forward new evidence as reveal the weakness of his opponent's position. We shall now move away from argumentative writing, where a clash of viewpoints provides the starting point for the author's argument, and proceed to consider a passage in which the author's opinions are presented to the reader in order to give him fresh insight into a subject, this new insight being largely the result of an appeal to the reader's feeling for the subject.

Appreciation and opinion

Most people's opinions on general topics, such as politics, religion, what is a good or bad film or book, etc., are not founded upon a simple, logical process of argument which leads them automatically to certain conclusions and the forming of their opinions on the matter. Thought and argument must obviously come into the process of your arriving at a definite opinion on, say, a particular film, but you are likely to be influenced by a host of things that relate to your feelings rather than to your more strictly logical thoughts about the film. There are, of course, the rather general factors, such as whether or not you were feeling good when you saw the film and the extent to which you were able to concentrate upon it and respond fully to it, and these are likely to depend on the more important factor – whether or not you had had previous experience of similar films which had formed your taste so that you brought to the film certain expectations which were either satisfied or not. Your final opinion of the film is likely to have arisen from a mesh of experience which includes an almost infinite possible range of associations and feelings combined with thought, and this is likely to be the way in which you arrive at an opinion on any work of art or indeed on any general matter.

It is, therefore, very often the case that a writer, wishing to communicate his opinion about, say, a work of art, will lead the reader through a process of appreciating the work of art before he offers his opinion or judgement of it. What I am introducing here is a type of writing which, though primarily concerned to arrive at a statement of opinion or the making of a judgement, can only do so effectively and convincingly if it includes a great deal of background material. This background material gives the reader at least a taste of the experience the writer has had. Out of that experience he has formed his judgement and, in his writing, he invites the reader to follow the same process of appreciation leading to the forming of an opinion.

The passage that follows is from a book of literary criticism, called *The Modern Writer and His World* by G. S. Fraser. The passage itself deals with a single literary work, the well-known play by Arnold Wesker called *Roots*. Fraser has already discussed the trilogy (or connected sequence of three plays) of which this is one and he commences his discussion of *Roots* with the judgement most commonly accorded to it, that it is the best of the three plays. He briefly indicates the lines along which he would support this judgement and then proceeds to give the plot of the play in such a manner as to convey not only information about it but also something of the dramatic quality that would be appreciated in the theatre. Out of this arise some comments on the main theme of the play, a theme which Fraser clearly believes to be of considerable significance in the modern world. Finally, a brief estimate or judgement of Wesker's success in portraying this particular human situation concludes the discussion of the play.

The structure of this paragraph (the whole discussion of the play is contained in a single paragraph) is what we might expect of any piece of writing dealing with ideas. It starts with a general statement, a synthesis, and then goes into a fairly detailed analysis of the material, the supporting evidence for the thesis, this evidence being, of course, the play itself. In the course of this analysis, Fraser emphasises those aspects and parts of the play that he thinks are of particular significance and relevance to his view of the work. After this detailed treatment, he is able to return naturally to his starting point, his estimate of the value of the play and to restate his opinion in rather more precise terms as a result of the preceeding analysis. However, the point I want to emphasise here is that the reader is unlikely to accept that final evaluation of the play if he has not been convinced by the preceding account of it and that account will work not essentially by presenting evidence, coldly as in a court of law, but by conveying something of the writer's own enthusiasm and feeling for the play. The reader is led through an organised process of appreciation.

The questions that follow the extract will help you to grasp the way in which this passage works. Suggested answers may be found on page 217.

Roots is regarded by most people as the most successful of these three plays, and I think the reason is that Wesker has translated his theme here not, as in the other two plays, into episodes stretching over a number of years, but into one tight
5   and unified dramatic situation. Briefly, the story is this. Beatie Bryant, who has been working in London as a waitress and has fallen in love with Ronnie Kahn, and with his cultural line of talk, comes back to visit her family in a Norfolk village. She has never met anybody like Ronnie before and his words are
10   constantly on her lips. She quotes him on everything, and he seems to have pontificated on everything – comics, football, the Bomb, Trade Unions, painting, music, politics, culture, his idea of the good life, in fact. This constant quoting of Ronnie's words is a subtle device. It makes us see Ronnie
15   through Beatie's dazzled and bewildered eyes and the pompous pronouncements that would be intolerable from him are bearable and even touching when repeated, perhaps without real understanding but with real love, by her. Most of the play is taken up with Beatie's half-comic and half-pathetic
20   efforts to sell her family 'culture'. There is something childlike about her enthusiasm that makes her preaching forgivable. Even while she is standing on a chair, addressing her mother as if she were at a public meeting, she is caught off her guard by a cloud of wasps and excitedly joins in a
25   wasp-hunt with her mother. Wesker shows her enjoying ice-cream and home-made bread, wallowing in her bath, and wanting to rush out and see a new litter of pigs. Her desperate attempt to get her family interested in ideas and music must, of course, come to little. They are prepared, however, to
30   welcome Ronnie. A magnificent spread has been prepared for

him — tomatoes, cheese, pickles, sausage rolls, tinned fruit, the whole works. He does not arrive, and Beatie is growing nervous. The family situation gets tenser and tenser, with Beatie trying to impress a growingly bored family, and finally

35 the postman comes with a pompous letter from Ronnie, breaking the whole thing off. Of course, Beatie is shattered and her family react badly. In her despair, Beatie confesses that she has been too lazy ever to learn anything from Ronnie; that she has merely been parroting him. She storms at her

40 mother, who slaps her face and says: "You say you know something we don't, so why don't you do the talking? Talk — go on, talk, gal." Beatie says she cannot, because she has no roots, she is "just a mass o' nothin'". And then suddenly eloquence comes to her. She talks suddenly out of her own

45 pain about how the mental laziness of the workers does, in fact, invite commercial artists to exploit them and true artists to despise them. Nobody is listening, but Beatie realises that at last she is not echoing Ronnie, not copying, but creating: her own thoughts are coming at last out of her own life. This

50 is a grand moment in the contemporary theatre, and Joan Plowright, with her sudden dance of triumph at this climax, bringing rough art and natural strength together, suddenly gave symbolic actuality to the theme that had been so much, and sometimes rather abstractly, talked around all through

55 the play. The theme of the almost blind striving of the culturally dispossessed to break through inner barricades, to learn to trust their own spontaneity, is vitally topical. At the same time, it should be noted . . . that knowing how to make home-made bread, how to prepare a grand high tea, with cold

60 meats and scones and jellies, or how to look after pigs, how to handle proverbial and colloquial language, all these things are in a wider sense part of "culture", too. Culture is not merely abstract ideas and literature, music and art. Are Beatie's family — their instinct that her Ronnie-ideas were second-

65 hand was not unsound — quite so barbarian after all? Wesker depicts them realistically, but not unsympathetically.

1. Put in your own words the reason why Fraser thinks that *Roots* is better than the other two plays in the trilogy (lines 1–5)?

2. Explain fully why Beatie's constant quoting of Ronnie's words is 'a subtle device'.

3. For what reason does Fraser mention the incident of the wasp-hunt (line 24)?

4. What do you understand to be the main cause of friction between Beatie and her family according to G. S. Fraser?

5. What evidence is there in this account of the play to indicate that the author finds Beatie an attractive character?

6. What event provokes the crisis point in the play?

7. Fraser explains Beatie's outburst as coming 'suddenly out of her own pain' (line 44):
   (a) what 'pain' do you think she is experiencing at this point in the play?
   (b) in lines 44–7, Fraser summarises the content of Beatie's outburst. Explain how the content of her speech is closely related to her own experience.

8. By commenting closely on lines 49–55, show why Fraser thinks that Joan Plowright's performance as Beatie is particularly worthy of mention.

9. Put into your own words what this author believes to be the main theme of the play (lines 55–7).

10. Say what you think Fraser's view of culture 'in a wider sense' (line 62) means.

As you will have realised, this is a complex piece of writing that makes its impact on the reader in various ways. Having studied the passage, it is worth while looking carefully at the various demands it makes upon us. You might not be faced with a piece very similar to this in the examination but, nevertheless, it is important that you should be able to approach any piece of writing with a general awareness of what demands might be made upon you if you are to respond to it fully. It is a question of coming to the examination with a sense of the varied responses that might possibly be required so that you can swiftly attune yourself to the demands of the passages that you find in the paper.

To begin with, we are asked to consider a judgement on the play, the author's opinion that *Roots* is a good play because it contains a 'tight and unified dramatic situation'. We are asked to entertain an abstract notion.

Secondly, we are presented with the story, the plot of the play. This is part of the evidence and background to support Fraser's initial assertion of the play's worth, and we must consider the impact that this story has upon us. The effect it creates is, in fact, largely determined by the way in which Fraser tells the story. For example, he conveys a great deal of sympathy with the main character, Beatie, refers to her 'dazzled and bewildered eyes', to her 'real love' for Ronnie, to the 'touching' way she repeats his ideas and to her natural spontaneity and humanity. All this constitutes an appeal to our feelings. We feel sorry for her, realising that she is infatuated with Ronnie and must be very hurt when he fails to turn up at her home. Of course, our feelings whilst reading this passage are only a shadow of what we might expect to feel when seeing the play in the theatre but, nevertheless, Fraser gives enough stimulation to our feelings for us to be able to appreciate the play's impact in the theatre even if we cannot experience it fully.

Thirdly, we have to respond to material in the passage which is analysis of the themes in the play, reasons why we should consider the climax to be particularly good theatre. Fraser draws from his description of the plot and its climax a statement of the theme or underlying ideas behind the action. He suggests that the play explores the meaning of culture and that it exposes the falseness of pretending to be 'educated' or 'cultured' or alive to ideas when this education, culture and these ideas have not grown naturally from a person's experience. Beatie only becomes truly cultured when she discovers her own ideas, grounded in the experience of being rejected by Ronnie and misunderstood by her family. What she says about the mental laziness of the workers refers as much to her as to other people, and she knows that. Fraser also suggests that her family have a natural culture of their own which consists of practical knowledge and ability to use country products and a sort of fundamental human understanding that enables them to see through her 'Ronnie-ideas'. This thematic analysis in the extract, this discussion of 'culture', demands of the reader a capacity for thinking and a serious concern about the issues under discussion. If you do not think this is an important question, then you are unlikely to feel that the play is of much significance.

To sum up, the grounds upon which Fraser bases his assertion that this is a good play are its capacity to evoke our sympathy for the characters, especially Beatie, the fact that it deals with an important issue in an age much concerned with education and the forcefulness with which it conveys this issue and explores its implications in the action of the drama. Fraser requires the reader, therefore, to respond with thought and feeling to his discussion of the play and to bring to a reading of this extract a serious concern for the cultural issues which arise in his discussion.

Summary of key points and rules in chapter 4

1. In approaching passages which contain argument, opinion or explanation, you need to concentrate on the main lines of the writer's thought.

2. This involves a thoughtful rather than imaginative concentration. You must distinguish the main points in the argument and see how the rest of the material is related to these main points.

3. There are two fundamental processes of thought at work in any passage of abstract argument. These processes are analysis and synthesis. Analysis is the breaking down of the subject-material into smaller details so that certain aspects of it may be emphasised. Synthesis is creating a pattern out of these significant details, creating an interpretation, a set of coherent generalisations.

4. A main idea may well be introduced obliquely: for example, it may be stated after the author has presented and rejected a possible interpretation of his material.

5. An extension of this occurs when the writer is setting out to oppose a previous interpretation by re-examining the evidence. Here you must be sure that you understand both the original interpretation and the interpretation that the writer is now proposing and that you can distinguish between the two.

6. A writer presenting arguments and interpretation of evidence may be concerned to effect changes of attitude in his readers. This may involve him in attacking his reader and, in order to disguise this attack, he may use the presence of an imaginary objector, against whom he can direct his arguments.

7. Writing about opinions and making judgements is often a complex business which may involve an appeal to the reader's general ideas and concerns and may require him to respond with feeling as well as thought. In other words, always try to become aware of what the author expects from you, of the sort of attention that you need to give to his writing.

Chapter 5
Describing Places

Why write at all?

Why, indeed! That may well be the feeling when you are given a choice of essay topics and you attempt to produce a piece of writing to order. Each of the topics confronting you seems equally unappealing. You may feel that you have nothing to say and no way of finding anything to say. Demoralisation swiftly follows the first few attempts to scratch out a couple of sentences. Each sentence is added to the last with great effort and without any sense of inspiration, a dry drudgery. It is to be expected that what one writes in this mood will be read with as little enthusiasm by teacher or examiner as that with which it was written. The whole thing is a mere exercise and the best that can be said of it is that it may demonstrate that you are capable of setting down a sequence of sentences without making any gross grammatical errors.

Of course, what such a student is lacking is inspiration, excitement in creating a piece of writing that has coherence and when written will give pleasure to the reader or excite his interest. It sounds highflown to suggest that even in an O-level English exam. you need to write with inspiration but I do believe that to be the case. If you are able to make a start on your essay feeling that you have something interesting to say, something to explore and discover in the course of the writing, you will gather a sort of energy and momentum and new ideas will come to you as you write. You may stumble upon ideas that you had not thought would be relevant to the topic and you may remember descriptive details or situations from your own experience or from books you have read. All this may be woven into your writing, enriching it, enabling the reader to feel that he is reading something that has significance, containing real-life experience and real thought. In other words, you will be communicating, giving your reader something, a glimpse into a way of looking at life or at a place, or whatever you are writing about, that is distinctively yours. It is personal.

What I am here suggesting is that inspiration is not some mysterious unapproachable quality reserved for the very few gifted people. We may not all be equally inspired, equally capable of creating something new and vital but we all have a personal and individual way of looking at life that is ours and no one else's. In our general development, we need to become aware of our own ways of looking at life in order to become mature and establish our own identities, separate from others'. In exactly the same way, we need to include in our writing a part of ourselves if our readers are to feel that here is something distinctive, something worth reading. No one is interested in a person who is so conventional and lacking in personal opinion or outlook as to seem virtually made of cardboard and, similarly, no one is going to be interested in a piece of writing that is produced to order, a mere exercise in spinning out sentences without any drive to communicate something personal behind it. There is an obvious parallel with playing a musical instrument: it would be excessively tedious to listen to someone endlessly playing scales, afraid to tackle a piece of music that would require some interpretation, the introduction of some feeling and expression. And, it would be equally tedious to listen to someone playing music without any feeling, just mechanically.

I have said that writing is a means of communicating with other people. It may well be more subtle than talking because it gives you the chance to explore your own inner world of thoughts and feelings and to produce in a more leisurely way than you can when talking, a more formed, organised sequence of words. Viewed in this light, writing is a creative act and it becomes art when you give appropriate external form to the perceptions within you.

This process of creating a work of art, matching appropriate words to inner perceptions, involves making a sequence of decisions and choices. If you were to look into your mind over the length of time that it takes to write an essay, you would find a whirling mass of ideas, some half-formed and fragmentary, others complete; you would find feelings and associations of feelings; and you would find a mass of sense-impressions, both of the things which may be seen, heard, smelt, touched and tasted in the present and of past experiences, memories clear or indistinct. In the process of writing you hunt through all this potential material, choosing the details that are to be combined in the essay. Every new word you write on the page in front of you is the product of a complex sifting, choosing process and, if all your choosing is governed by an overall sense of what you are creating, of what you want to say, then you are producing a work of art, though indeed it may be quite humble and limited.

So, don't think of yourself as necessarily performing a mechanical exercise when you start writing. Whoever you are and however ordinary you may feel yourself to be, you know yourself to be an individual, subtly different from every other person on this planet, different because no one else has had exactly the same combination of background influences and experiences as you nor possesses the same style of perceiving experience. Make your writing, therefore, issue from your personal experience and your own thoughts. The more individual it is, the more satisfaction you will get from it and the more inspired you will feel when you are writing.

Start with the senses

Although I have emphasised that your writing must not be produced as a mere exercise, exercises do have a place in the development of the necessary skills of writing as they aid the growth of most skills of the body and mind. If you practise and master the simple techniques that I am going on to suggest, you will find them useful in two ways: you will often be able to make a start on your work, to get going, like the athlete who needs to limber up before he is ready to begin a race, and you will find that, in the course of writing an essay, you can often draw on the simple skills you have associated with exercises in order to enrich a particular section or carry yourself on to a further stage in the essay or story. The pianist uses the mastery of exercises in the same ways, limbering up beforehand with scales and having frequent recourse in the playing of a piece of music to basic techniques of agility which would have been mastered through practising exercises.

There are various exercises with which the budding writer can practise. In this chapter, however, we are mainly concerned with describing places and the first thing to learn in creating descriptions is the importance of the five senses. What follows should help you to utilise your sense of hearing to the maximum extent in your writing.

1. Sit comfortably and close your eyes. It does not matter where you are. Concentrate on everything you can hear however loud or quiet.

2. Concentrate on sounds you can hear outside the building you are in. Can you hear traffic, wind, rain, sounds of people calling,

of machines or animals? Isolate each particular sound and describe it to yourself. For example, I can, at the moment of first writing this book, hear traffic going along a main road about a quarter of a mile from my house. I might describe that noise as, 'a slight hum in the distance, which gradually becomes a louder purring, reaches a climax and then dies away. A moment later, there is a higher-pitched noise, approaching from a distance, following the same sequence of crescendo and then fading.' Describe in writing all the sounds that you can hear outside the building.

3. Listen with concentration for every sound within the building. Then write down what you can hear.

4. Concentrate again with closed eyes. Moving from the more distant sounds, gradually work closer until you are listening to the sounds inside the room in which you are sitting and then to any sounds that you can perceive in your own body, your breathing or the beating of your heart. Write down your perceptions.

5. Look over the material you have collected and write a paragraph combining the sounds you have identified in the order in which they have been perceived by you.

What you have written may not seem terribly inspired but, if you have concentrated thoroughly, you will have created in your paragraph a very precise sense of your surroundings; your description will have a clear structure and order since it will move from the distant to the very near; and you will have conveyed all this sense of the reality of your circumstances entirely through the use of one sense. Can you not see the potential, the multitude of ways in which you can develop and strengthen your writing simply by concentrating firmly on what you can hear, see, taste, smell, touch? Such perceptions may occur either in the actual place being described – as in the exercise above – or the reality of a place can be created through imagination and memory.

What follows is a selection of short passages, a poem and some suggestions for writing short pieces of description which will give you an opportunity to set your imagination free within fairly well-defined limits and to explore some possibilities for integrating into your writing something of that rich tissue of sense impressions that is so naturally a part of everyday life that we tend to take it for granted. Try to experiment and develop imaginative freedom and to combine that freedom with a close and concentrated attention to the details of description that you choose to work on.

A moment caught

That exercise is a way of fixing in writing the experience of a single moment as apprehended through only one sense. It may be expanded to include the other senses as, indeed, it is in the following poem which records a moment when a train stopped at a remote country station for no apparent reason.

> Adlestrop
>
> Yes. I remember Adlestrop –
> The name, because one afternoon
> Of heat the express-train drew up there
> Unwontedly. It was late June.
>
> The steam hissed. Someone cleared his throat.
> No one left and no one came
> On the bare platform. What I saw
> Was Adlestrop – only the name.
>
> And willows, willow-herb, and grass,
> And meadowsweet, and haycocks dry,
> No whit less still and lonely fair
> Than the high cloudlets in the sky.
>
> And for that minute a blackbird sang
> Close by, and round him, mistier,
> Farther and farther, all the birds
> Of Oxfordshire and Gloucestershire.
>
> *Edward Thomas*

First, establish clearly what is the sequence of events in this poem. It is a moment caught and recorded with great precision, a moment which had occurred somewhere in the past and is called to mind by the poet through some chance mention of the name, 'Adlestrop'. The hiss of steam and someone clearing his throat are the details the poet first clearly identifies of that moment in the little station, though, of course, the first verse is evocative of many impressions and thoughts especially for someone able to remember a similar experience in a steam-train – the windows down, the smell of the train, the slight discomfort of the hot carriage seats, the breeze against the face, etc. He looks out to see the bare platform, the odd name of the station, grass and wild flowers and, as he looks further away, the small haystacks in nearby fields. He looks up to see small clouds in the sky. Sight, in turn, gives way to sound and he becomes aware of a single blackbird singing close by and then of bird songs at increasing distances from him. Out of a few carefully selected sense impressions, a perfect little poem is created, the movement being from the immediate and close-at-hand out into the distance.

Create in your imagination a situation in which you are in motion, in a car, on a cycle or motor-cycle, and you suddenly stop for some reason which need not be elaborated. Imagine precisely where you are, in town, country, by the sea, etc. Draw upon your memories of a suitable place, any place, to elaborate in your mind exactly what you can see and hear. Then write a brief prose description in which you are able to recreate the contrast between sense impressions received in motion and those you perceive when you have stopped. You could allow your eye to move from details near at hand to those further away and similarly describe the most obvious, insistent sounds first before suggesting those coming from a distance or those that are quieter. Try to feel that you are leading your reader into the experience very accurately and precisely.

Hearing things

The narration of an unadorned sequence of events is frequently tedious both for writer and reader. Bringing them to life often involves conveying the substance of the happenings through the awareness of some character who observes them and very often the reader may be invited to experience the events as if he is seeing or hearing them along with the characters involved. The situation in the following extract is simple and requires little commentary: Jane has just given birth and is waiting with the doctor and midwife for her cousin, Lucy, to arrive. Notice how the sequence of ordinary events downstairs is mediated to the reader through Lucy's sense of hearing.

When the doctor had finished his cup of tea, he looked at his watch and said that he must go: the midwife said that she would stay until Lucy arrived to relieve her vigil; but even as the doctor went down the stairs Jane heard the car draw up outside and knew that Lucy was there. The doctor let her in:

she could hear them exchanging remarks in the hall, and could hear the dry murmur and cough that indicated the presence of James, Lucy's husband.

'That must be my cousin,' said Jane to the midwife . . .

'I'll be off, then,' said the midwife, who had already risen to her feet and was donning the layers of cardigan which the heat of the room had obliged her to cast off. 'I'll be back in the morning, nine o'clock.'

'Yes,' said Jane.

And the woman left: she met James and Lucy on the stairs, and Jane could hear another low-pitched indistinct murmur of greeting and parting, and then the dividing of their footsteps, the opening and closing of the front door downstairs, and then the tap and push upon her own – and then there, suddenly, was Lucy, like a visitor from another life, her arms full of parcels, a blank, diffuse and nervous smile upon her face.

There are a number of writing exercises that you can probably devise by using this extract from *The Waterfall*, by Margaret Drabble, as a model and by considering the problems of narrating occurrences through the perceptions of characters involved in or witness to those occurrences. One point to bear in mind is the necessity for strictly maintaining adherence to a single point of observation, just as in drawing, the laws of perspective must be maintained if the artist is to present a realistic view. In writing from a single angle of vision, it is important to fully 'realise' in your imagination the position and awareness of the character who is your medium for apprehending the events.

1. You could pattern a piece of writing in a similar form to that of the extract from *The Waterfall*, imagining yourself or someone else lying ill in bed, listening to the sounds of people moving about the house and reconstructing their actions. A pleasing and delicate element in the passage above is the sudden appearance of Lucy, 'like a visitor from another life'. As sound impressions give way to sight, we realise just how cut-off from the ordinary world Jane was feeling during the traumatic event of the birth of

her child. Perhaps you can incorporate a similar movement from sound to sight.

2. You could write up an incident when someone refuses to open the door to a visitor. Either the visitor hears a sequence of sounds from inside the room which suggests to him a sequence of events or the person inside the room could speculate, on the evidence of the sounds he hears, as to the identity of the visitor. With a bit of ingenuity you might even combine the two and write about the same sequence of events as perceived from two different angles.

3. Develop a few paragraphs using sounds to show what happens when a room full of people is suddenly plunged into darkness through a power-cut. Make sure you hear the events through one character's ears.

Snapshots

We probably use the sense of sight more than any other in descriptive writing. What follows are some simple exercises for developing your capacity for focusing on visual details within the limits imposed by a single glance or view. As in the section above, 'A moment caught', the aim here is to convey with a few deft strokes, the exact pictorial quality of what one can see at any particular moment. If you can develop the skill of using an imaginative eye in your writing, you will find yourself able to bring to life what might otherwise seem dreary and unrewarding material. This short extract from the volume of Maxim Gorky's autobiography, called *My Apprenticeship*, suggests some five-finger exercises in what might be called snapshot description.

In the more remote streets, however, I was able to look into the windows in the lower storeys of houses, if they were not too heavily frosted over or hung with curtains. Those windows revealed many different activities. I saw people praying, kissing, fighting, playing cards, chattering away in anxious, hollow-sounding voices. A mute, fish-like life opened up in front of me—just as though I had put a kopek in a slot-machine.

In a cellar I saw two women sitting at a table, one younger than the other. Opposite them a long-haired schoolboy was reading to them and waving his arm about. The younger woman had a dark frown on her face as she listened and leaned back in her chair. The older one, who was slim and whose hair was very thick, suddenly covered her face with her hands, and her shoulders trembled. The schoolboy threw the book down and when the younger woman had leaped to her feet and fled from the room, he fell on his knees and started kissing the other one's hands.

Through another window I could see a large bearded man rocking on his knees a woman who was wearing a red jacket — just as though she were a child. I could tell he was singing as his mouth was wide open and his eyes were bulging. The woman was shaking with laughter and threw herself backwards. The man stopped, sat her up straight and started singing again which made her laugh all the more.

In this 'mute, fish-like life', seen, as it were, in a slot-machine, sight is the only one of the five senses available to Gorky and so we are presented with two delightfully unexplained glimpses into peoples' lives. The relationship between the two women and the schoolboy and the reasons for their displays of feelings are a matter for speculation. Gorky does not indulge in speculation but simply describes what he sees and so the emotional content of the situation is highlighted and rendered all the more intriguing. The man in the other scene is reckoned to be singing only because of the appearance of his face — 'his mouth was wide open and his eyes were bulging': the visual detail is strengthened because there is no sound. Consider the overall effect of this passage; it conveys a curiously grotesque and flat view of these people because everything is mediated to the reader through the eyes alone of the narrator. It is a good indication of what might be achieved by being pointedly aware of visual sense impressions.

1. Describe what you see through the open curtains of a window when you are walking past at night. It may not be only people that come to mind as you think about such a momentary experience. Try to visualise the colours of the room, its furniture, decorations, etc.

2. You have been asleep in the open air somewhere. You wake. Describe the first things you see before you are quite sure of where you are.

3. What meets your eyes as you enter a room at home, at school or in a public building? Is the room crowded, empty, or containing only one person? Is it light or dark, colourful or drab? And so on ... the possibilities are endless and it hardly matters at all what you choose as material on which to sharpen your descriptive powers. All that is important is that you should clearly visualise your subject and make sure that your reader can also see it.

How to develop your descriptions

The spirit of a place

I have up to now in this chapter been presenting ways of improving your writing which depend essentially on awareness of your sense impressions and ability to concentrate with great precision on what might be perceived in a brief moment. This use of detail should become habitual and will give a 'three-dimensional' quality to your writing, so that what you are describing will seem to have been really experienced either in actuality or in the imagination. A number of the exercises above move a little beyond the immediate and already suggest some ways of developing descriptions beyond merely cataloguing details. For example, the poem 'Adlestrop' moves away from the immediate spot to convey a feeling of distance, so that one nearby blackbird becomes representative of the thousands of birds in Oxfordshire and Gloucestershire. One way, therefore, of developing descriptions is to move from the specific which is precisely described to the more general, to convey in broader terms perhaps the spirit or atmosphere of a place.

The passage from Gorky's *My Apprenticeship* on pages 101–2 occurs in a section of his autobiography in which he describes how, as a youth, he wandered the streets of his town at night. The following two paragraphs are taken from the same section and constitute a good example of the way an author may convey the atmosphere or spirit of a place through a selection of typical details. In the first paragraph, he reminisces generally about his noctural wanderings and remembers the sort of things that he usually noticed. Then, in the second paragraph, he concentrates on one particular memory and so focuses the atmosphere.

> On calmer nights, I loved walking around the town more than anything else, from street to street, ending up in the

most deserted places. At times I seemed to be flying along, as lonely as the moon in the sky. My shadow glided on before me falling over glinting patches of snow and comically bumping into stones or fences. The night-watchman would pace down the middle of the street, wearing a heavy sheepskin coat and carrying a rattle, while his dog jogged along beside him . . . Sometimes I passed cheerful girls with their boyfriends and I thought that they had escaped evening service like me. Sometimes peculiar smells drifted from brightly-lit casement windows into the pure air — fine, unfamiliar smells that hinted of a life that I knew nothing about. I would stand under a window, sniff hard and try to guess what kind of life people led in those houses, what they were like. They should have been going to mass but they were all having a gay, noisy time instead, laughing and playing some special kind of guitar, and the air was filled with the rich metallic twanging of their strings.

A single-storeyed, squat-looking house on the corner of the deserted Tikhonovsky and Martynovsky streets particularly caught my attention. I discovered it one moonlit night, just before Shrovetide, when the thaw had set in. Strange sounds blended with the warm air and poured in a single stream from a window ventilator. It was as though a very strong and good-natured person were singing without opening his mouth; I could not make out the words, but the song was very familiar and easy to follow, although that irritating twanging which interrupted the even flow made it rather more difficult to follow. I sat on the kerb and came to the conclusion that someone was playing an incredibly powerful violin — so powerful that it hurt just listening to it. Sometimes it grew so loud that the whole house appeared to be shaking and the window panes rattled in their frames. Melting snow trickled down from the roof — and tears streamed from my face.

As an exercise in more developed descriptive writing, try to construct a few paragraphs in which you convey the atmosphere of a place both by using details which would be typical of any visit to the spot and by including some specific reminiscence. This is a slightly more sophisticated mode of writing than would be demanded by the exercises in using sense impressions and it requires a more obvious choice of different kinds of material.

1. Choose your place (your own town at night, in the early morning, during the rush hour; a place you know well from holiday visits, etc. – the possibilities are as extensive as has been your own experience) and allow your imagination to expand, remembering and envisaging all that is characteristic of the place and what gives it significance for you.

2. Then, select a manageable number of typical aspects (like Gorky's observations of his shadow, the night-watchman, cheerful girls with their boyfriends, smells coming from the houses) and work them into a general description.

3. Finally, you might care to concentrate on some particular incident which happened, or you could imagine happening, there and which will summarise and convey your feelings about the place.

When you have finished the piece of writing I have just suggested, you could look over it again from a slightly different point of view. I emphasised the necessity for realising the place in your imagination before writing and the importance of choosing material – events or descriptive details – carefully in the process of writing. A question arises: on what basis did you choose the material you included? Was there an overriding feeling about the place that determined your choice or perhaps a particular effect that you wanted to create? For example, had you chosen to write about a place where, as a child, you habitually took happy summer seaside holidays, you might have included details that convey bustle and pleasure, people enjoying themselves in a carefree, happy manner and, if you focused in on a particular, characteristic event, you would probably have recalled or imaginatively created an occasion in which you experienced these pleasurable feelings. There may even be, in such a piece, an element of nostalgia, regret that such things are not any longer easily accessible for you.

Such a piece as this would contrast with the passage from Gorky's autobiography, where the overriding feeling that infuses the spirit of the place – the town at night – is created out of the contrast between the people having a 'gay, noisy time' in the houses he passes and his own feeling of being excluded from this carefree pleasure. It is a complex 'spirit' that emerges from a careful reading of this passage: on the one hand, he asserts that he loved walking around the town and 'ending up in the most deserted places' whilst, on the other hand, he writes 'tears streamed from my face' at the end of this extract. I daresay most people have experienced some such emotional state of being happy in their own melancholy or of emotional release as a result of escaping from the drudgery of ordinary life. It must be common enough to have some reaction to the sight of 'cheerful girls with their boyfriends' when one is walking alone and conscious of being isolated. Here, however, Gorky seems to relish seeing the couples, to feel that they, like him, have escaped from some dreary duty like evening service and so he, through seeing them, takes some of their pleasure into himself.

For our purposes, it does not matter too much how we would describe Gorky's emotional state or the effect of this particular passage. The point I want to make and to emphasise here is that one way of developing a description and conveying the spirit or atmosphere of a place is to have a distinct range of feelings associated with it. In other words, come into relationship with your chosen place and then that relationship will determine your choice of descriptive material and will ensure that a unifying atmosphere emerges. A developed description cannot be a random choice of arbitrarily-chosen details. Gorky includes the 'cheerful girls' because his observation of them is intimately related to his overall feelings about the streets of the town at night.

Another example of a description where the narrator's relationship with a place infuses his writing with a unifying spirit occurs towards the end of Joseph Conrad's short story, 'Youth'. The narrative concerns a ship caught and wrecked in a storm and the escape of the men in small boats. They drift for some time and eventually arrive at a port in the East during the night. They sleep in their boats exhausted. The story is narrated by an old man recalling these events and in the following extract he describes his first impressions when he opened his eyes in the morning . . .

"But when I opened my eyes again the silence was as complete as though it had never been broken. I was lying in a flood of light, and the sky had never looked so far, so high, before. I opened my eyes and lay without moving.

"And then I saw the men of the East – they were looking at me. The whole length of the jetty was full of people. I saw brown, bronze, yellow faces, the black eyes, the glitter of an

Eastern crowd. And all these beings stared without a murmur, without a sigh, without a movement. They stared down at the boats, at the sleeping men who at night had come to them from the sea. Nothing moved. The fronds of palms stood still against the sky. Not a branch stirred along the shore, and the brown roofs of hidden houses peeped through the green foliage, through the big leaves that hung shining and still like leaves forged of heavy metal. This was the East of the ancient navigators, so old, so mysterious, resplendent and sombre, living and unchanged, full of danger and promise. And these were the men. I sat up suddenly. A wave of movement passed through the crowd from end to end, passed along the heads, swayed the bodies, ran along the jetty like a ripple on the water, like a breath of wind on a field – and all was still again. I see it now – the wide sweep of the bay, the glittering sands, the wealth of green infinite and varied, the sea blue like the sea of a dream, the crowd of attentive faces, the blaze of vivid colour – the water reflecting it all, the curve of the shore, the jetty, the high-sterned outlandish craft floating still, and the three boats with the tired men from the West sleeping, unconscious of the land and the people and of the violence of the sunshine. They slept thrown across the thwarts, curled on bottom-boards, in the careless attitudes of death. The head of the old skipper, leaning back in the stern of the long-boat, had fallen on his breast, and he looked as though he would never wake. Farther out old Mahon's face was upturned to the sky, with the long white beard spread out on his breast, as though he had been shot where he sat at the tiller; and a man, all in a heap in the bows of the boat, slept with both arms embracing the stem-head and with his cheek laid on the gunwale. The East looked at them without a sound."

This is an extraordinarily fine piece of writing, powerful and clear as it gathers itself towards that last, simple sentence which summarises the one aspect of the memory that the narrator has time and again returned to in the course of the description. The stillness and silence of his first experience of the East held promise, romance and seemed a challenge to his youth. The silence is so strong, so much a presence in the scene that the reader can virtually hear it.

Conrad is able to imply great depths of significance and mystery in this timeless moment of stillness. This is created partly by the nature of the situation: the fugitive Westerners at last finding safety and a young man, full of ideas and feelings about the East, at last confronting it in reality. We are aware that behind this line of people on the jetty and the cluster of houses beyond lies the infinite variety of a great continent full of unknown cultures. It is the youth's sense of touching upon the mysterious, vast unknown that gives the passage its strange undercurrent of excitement. He is, of course, still in the boat, looking at the East. He has communicated with it only in the sense that the men moved when he sat up in the boat. So, he can make this immediate vision of an obscure seaboard town stand for half the world. The power of the passage, then, depends to a large extent on the unusually potent relationship that the young man has with this place, a relationship that is built not on familiarity but on fantasy and expectation. It is the sort of encounter with a place that happens but once in a lifetime or never at all and if you have such a memory to work on in your writing or can conceive of an experience with as much unique significance, you will be fortunate indeed.

However, there is more here of interest to the writer, even if he is only practising ways of describing places, than the content alone. The way in which the description is paced, the way it moves and develops, deserves attention. The narrator's first impression when he opens his eyes is simple and general, just a flood of light and the sky. He sees men on the jetty and describes them in the most general terms. They are representative, not specific; they are any eastern crowd, standing for all the men of the East. He has mentioned the lack of movement and, after isolating that fact in the short statement, 'Nothing moved', he looks further off at the palms, at glimpses of houses, at the leaves of the trees. Conrad uses these details to extend and emphasise the stillness. They are there conveying the narrator's overwhelming impression of the place; they are not just arbitrary details thrown in. Hence too, the comparison of the leaves to 'leaves forged of heavy metal'. The comparison emphasises this weighty stillness that the young man feels and it also suggests something ancient and strangely artificial, as that scene on the jetty must have seemed to him. It works in the same way as the later comparison of the blue sea 'like the sea of a dream'. These comparisons get inside the young man's mind and feelings, enabling us to appreciate his sense of unreality and his astonished realisation that here, indeed, is the East. Because he has not yet encountered it, it still seems artificial, a dream. It is worth stressing, at this point, that if you elaborate your description by using comparisons, they should somehow convey or reinforce the overall feelings in the piece of writing. They should never be thought of as merely opportunities for exercising ingenuity.

With a masterly stroke, Conrad develops his description by creating a distinct moment: the young man sits up and there is a ripple of consequent movement along the jetty. What is the effect of introducing this detail of movement into a static scene? The place, I think, seems all the more extraordinarily still and quiet when the movement has ceased. By contrast, this ripple of response emphasises the strange static appearance of the scene.

After that, the description again changes its tone and a new effect is introduced by the phrase, 'I see it now –'. We are suddenly reminded that all this has happened in the past and so the scene becomes less immediate, less totally absorbing. It is as if the description is in two stages: to begin with, we are with the amazed young man, sharing his feelings about the strange scene before his eyes and, then, after we have been reminded that half a lifetime has passed since this event occurred, we share the feelings of an older man who looks at the scene from a more distant standpoint. He takes a wide, sweeping view of the place and then focuses on details describing the Westerners asleep in their boats. It is natural that he should describe them in detail: this is his much-known western world; the East remains generalised, an impression rather than a detailed description.

Many points have emerged in the course of looking at this passage. I have included it because it illustrates just how complex an art is descriptive writing and how much care you must take if you are to produce description that will give something of worth to your readers. Try to be sensitive to the variety and range of your feelings about a place; try to be aware of what in a place is of general impact for you and choose ways of expressing yourself that convey the generalised nature of the impression you want to create; when certain aspects seem to you to be more immediate or knowable, in the way that the Westerners were to Conrad's narrator, then provide sufficient detail to convey the picture you have in mind. Finally, decide on an order for including these different sorts of material so that you will give a shape and overall structure to your description.

This passage does not easily suggest mere exercises in writing. You may, however, care to develop a similar situation in which you encounter, for the first time, some place about which you had previously had many thoughts and fantasies. Another possibility is to write about somewhere which you first of all see in the present and which you afterwards remember about: the first half of your description could be immediate, the things that strike your senses at the moment of first perceiving them, and then you could set the whole experience back in time and provide a more detached, generalised description. A similar effect could be created by describing a town, for example, from the point of view of someone who is walking in it and then from the point of view of someone who sees it from a distant hill or from an aeroplane.

Summary of key points and rules in chapter 5

1. Be aware that you have a personal way of looking at things and aim to communicate your personal vision in your writing.

2. Never be mechanical in writing: choose every detail you include and, if possible, know why you have chosen it.

3. In any piece of descriptive writing, use your senses. What did you see, hear, smell, etc? If you are not writing from memory, ask yourself what sense impressions you can imagine perceiving in the place you have chosen to write about.

4. Develop your descriptions by using different kinds of material, moving from the specific to the general, or *vice versa*, or by alternating between particular details and more general characteristic impressions.

5. Above all, come into relationship with any place that you describe, have feelings about it and be sensitive to the variety and range of your feelings. Your relationship with a place may well govern your choice of detail for inclusion in the description and the order in which the material is presented.

6. Finally, never forget your reader. Give him the pleasure of being invited into your personal reactions to and feelings about whatever you are describing.

Essay questions

In conclusion, here is a selection of essay questions recently set by different examination boards for Ordinary-level English Language. When you first look at them, some might seem to be far removed from the writing you have done in working through this chapter. With more careful consideration, you will see that the description of a place could be an important part of any one of these essays. Think out how they might be developed.

1. Describe a day you dreaded which eventually turned out all right, or a day you looked forward to eagerly which proved a big disappointment.

2. Imagine you have run away from home or from school. Write a letter to someone in your family or in school, describing your present circumstances and explaining the reasons for what you have done.

3. Do you prefer to travel by air or to travel by rail and sea?

4. Where in the world would you most like to live and why?

5. Describe the scene and give your thoughts as an observer of a Rag Day or a local carnival or a procession or a Wakes Week celebration.

6. Describe what you see and what your thoughts are when visiting a scrapbreaker's yard or an old junk shop.

Chapter 6
Writing about People

One thing that we must face concerning composition questions on Ordinary-level English Language papers is their invariable appearance of bleakness. They are necessarily bleak in the interests of brevity but the result of their brevity is that all the imaginative stimulus and all the development of thought to carry you into the topic has to be found within you; and it is not so easy to suddenly conceive of a developed and vibrant response to a question that, at first sight, seems so bleak. In the stressful conditions of the examination room, with his friends scribbling madly around him, the average candidate may well feel daunted by questions like the following, both of which have recently been set by different examination boards:

Describe two of your friends who have contrasting qualities.

Each form in a school tends to develop its own special characteristics: it also tends to have its own characters, two or three people well known to the staff and to the rest of the school. Write about your impressions of your form and its characters.

You have read through the paper, chosen perhaps a question like one of these and now it is up to you. Out of thin air, apparently, you must conjure up something to say about people that you know, people that you have seen day-in and day-out for years and have come to know them and their characteristic ways of going about things so well that you have ceased to wonder about them or examine their personalities and motives and no longer try to work out precisely what effect they create in you. It may not always be true that familiarity breeds contempt but it does tend to lead to a routined and often dull response so that we cease to use our eyes and ears. Somehow we just 'know' our friends, family, relations and the people we work with; we accept them, like them or dislike them and, unless we are of an unusually analytical turn of mind, rarely make conscious statements about them to ourselves, or bother to register aspects of other people's characters that we intuitively accept.

It is not, therefore, surprising that the mind may go blank and you may feel that you have either nothing to say or nothing that is worth saying, when you are confronted with this type of essay topic. What you need at this point is a fresh, sharp view of the person about whom you are going to write. You need, in imagination, to experience that person with far greater intensity than is possible in the normal course of events. You need also to remember the obvious fact that your reader starts from scratch in getting to know your subject when he picks up your essay. All sorts of minor details and ways of behaving that may seem to you, from your position of far greater knowledge of the person in question, to be so trivial and unimportant as not to be worth describing, must be spelt out and will give life and reality to the portrait. In the course of a conversation about a mutual friend, one might well say, 'Of course, X reacted in his usual way. You know what he's like!' but if you were describing the event to someone who did not know your friend, then a far greater wealth of detail would be required. In approaching this sort of topic, therefore, you need to take a new and perceptive view of your subject and to be able to select and develop those characteristics which will give the reader the most convincing entry into the sense of knowing the person about whom you are writing.

There are ways of dealing with the vacancy that besets the best of us on contemplating such a task, questions that you might ask yourself which could lead you on into producing a well-organised and perceptive piece of writing, which may contain a variety of approaches and modes of describing your chosen subject. What do you mean when you say that you 'know' someone? You know what he looks like and what he wears; you know something of his habits and his moods and of the ways his moods affect his manner, of the way, for example, his face indicates that he is happy, angry or whatever; you will have experienced his reactions to different circumstances and, if you know him at all well, will have recognised that his reactions are in many ways subtly different from other people's; you will also know what his tastes are and the friends he chooses to know well.

This chapter has been designed to open up some of these possible approaches and, as in the previous chapter, I shall suggest some simple exercises in writing which will give you an entry into thinking more closely and perceptively about the topic you want to write on. As I have said before, it is important that, in the actual process of writing, you should feel that you are discovering something, that you are writing not in a dull manner about something which bores you and will therefore most certainly bore your reader, but that your composition is itself *exploratory*, a way of bringing together observations and thoughts that you had not combined in quite the same way ever before. When you have developed a skill of asking yourself questions that will lead you into exploring your own perceptions and *realising* them in your writing, then you will enjoy writing; you will feel you are getting somewhere and your reader or the examiner will share in this pleasurable excitement.

In the course of this chapter, I shall occasionally be referring back to chapter 2, 'Understanding People in Books'. You will find it helpful to read that chapter again, from a slightly different angle and considering how the techniques employed by the writers of the passages I quoted might assist you in developing your own styles of writing about people.

The sense of a character

External description

If you glance back at the two questions I quoted at the beginning of this chapter, you will notice that they both require more than merely objective descriptions of what people look like: they require more than a catalogue of visible details. The first talks of 'contrasting qualities' and the second asks you to look at your own 'impressions' of the form and its characters. Although your first thoughts are almost bound to involve concentrating on a visual image of the person you are going to write about, a straightforward description of his external appearance – the sort of description that the police provide in order to trace some wanted person – is not likely to take us very far into appreciating a character and the qualities that give a living sense of an identifiable person.

In fact, of course, it is almost impossible to describe the appearance of people without implying something about their personalities. Consider one of your friends. Let us say that he is short, dark with brown eyes, of medium build, with a pale complexion and big ears. The general specification suggests a faint outline picture of some sort but the moment we say, for example, that his hair is neatly cut and carefully combed or that it is frequently ruffled and untidy or that he starts the day looking spick and span and, because he is always passing his hand through his hair, it swiftly becomes less neat, we are beginning, by implication, to convey something about his personality. The moment we begin to be more precise and to depart from the police officer's press release, we begin to convey the sense of character.

Consider, then, the clothes your subject wears. Unless he has to wear a uniform which is specified down to the minutest detail, his choice of garments and their condition and his manner of wearing them are going to reflect his 'taste', his 'style' and, therefore, to provide a useful means of entry into appreciating his character. Words like style and taste reflect our belief in the uniqueness of each individual, for we do not believe, unless we are feeling extremely disillusioned with human existence, that people are random collections of details, arbitrarily compiled. Every time I put on a piece of clothing, I *choose* to do so and my manner of wearing it and its condition will reflect my personality, even if I did not choose to wear it in the first place. You may have to wear a school blazer and that may tend to minimise your individuality but whether or not you brush the dandruff off the collar or fill your pockets so that they bulge, or habitually rub your elbows on the table so that the cloth becomes shiny, or carefully remove particles of your dinner from the lapels will all, in some small degree, reveal your style, and hence your character.

I labour these points because it is vitally important, when you are describing someone, not to throw in arbitrary details simply in order to fill up the page. Every detail can count towards building up a picture that will either convince the reader that a real person is emerging or not.

As an initial five-finger exercise, write a paragraph or two which describes two people dressed in exactly the same way, two policemen walking the beat, two soldiers sitting on a train on the way back to camp, two boys or girls in school uniform. Your aim should be to convey a general impression of their dress in a few sentences and then to concentrate on those details which indicate that these people are individuals. Before you start writing, get clear in your own mind that these are two very different people, with different faces and mannerisms and try to convey in your writing their separate personalities.

First impressions

An exhaustively-detailed head-to-toe description is not only tedious to write: it is untrue to the way in which we habitually perceive people. At an initial meeting with someone, you are more likely to gain first a general impression of him or her, in terms of his background and appearance and the context in which you have met, and then to react to or notice some particular detail, that he has a curious way of smiling, or of gesturing with his hand or of moving about. When you present a character to your reader in a composition, you should bear this in mind. Your reader will be meeting someone for the first time, he will be encountering a stranger, and your description will convince him of the reality of this stranger if the presentation mirrors the process that occurs in real life, of encountering and responding to a new person.

We can learn a great deal about the various ways in which characters may be introduced by looking at a few short extracts from novels but an important complicating factor enters as soon as we start considering the way strangers are introduced into a novel. Since novels are invariably about the relationships between people, we are often interested not merely in the stranger himself but also in the effect that the stranger has upon the characters we already know. The stranger's appearance and impact is likely to be mediated to the reader through the eyes of some other character or characters and they will respond to the new person in the light of their perception of him and the feelings he evokes. In the same way, when you are writing about someone else, you will be enabling your reader to see the new person through your eyes and will be selecting those aspects of his appearance and habitual actions that have made a strong impression on you. If you have a clear sense of what is characteristic of your subject, you will be able to communicate that response successfully to the reader.

What we therefore have to consider is how you may set about focusing your reaction to someone you either know well or are meeting for the first time so that your introduction of this stranger to the reader is not a catalogue of random details but conveys a coherent impression.

Let us start with an extract from D. H. Lawrence's short story *The Fox*. The passage describes the entry of a stranger who arrives unexpectedly at a farm which is being run by two girls, always refered to by their surnames, March and Banford.

    "Hello!"

    March recoiled, and took a gun from a corner.

5   "What do you want?" she cried, in a sharp voice.

Again the soft, softly-vibrating man's voice said:

"Hello! What's wrong?"

10   "I shall shoot!" cried March. "What do you want?"

"Why, what's wrong? What's wrong?" came the soft, wondering, rather scared voice: and a young soldier, with his heavy kit on his back, advanced into the dim light.

15

"Why," he said, "who lives here then?"

"We live here," said March. "What do you want?"

20   "Oh!" came the long, melodious, wonder-note from the young soldier. "Doesn't William Grenfel live here then?"

"No—you know he doesn't."

25   "Do I? Do I? I don't, you see. He *did* live here, because he was my grandfather, and I lived here myself five years ago. What's become of him then?

The young man — or youth, for he would not be more than
30 twenty — now advanced and stood in the inner doorway. March, already under the influence of his strange, soft, modulated voice, stared at him spellbound. He had a ruddy, roundish face, with fairish hair, rather long, flattened to his forehead with sweat. His eyes were blue, and very bright and
35 sharp. On his cheeks, on the fresh ruddy skin were fine, fair hairs, like a down, but sharper. It gave him a slightly glistening look. Having his heavy sack on his shoulders, he stooped, thrusting his head forward. His hat was loose in one hand. He stared brightly, very keenly from girl to girl,
40 particularly at March, who stood pale, with great dilated eyes, in her belted coat and puttees, her hair knotted in a big crisp knot behind. She still had the gun in her hand. Behind her, Banford, clinging to the sofa-arm, was shrinking away, with half-averted head.

There is much that we can learn from this passage. To begin with, notice the subtlety with which the young man gradually becomes present on the scene: at first, he is but a voice, then 'a young soldier' perceived in the dim light of the porch and, finally, his appearance is clearly seen as he advances into the inner doorway. The entry is placed clearly in a situation and it is dramatic in the sense that we could envisage the movement taking place on a stage. You might bear in mind the possibility of creating such a gradual entry for a character into your writing; the sound of a voice could give way to the sight of a person, a casual glimpse one day could be followed by a proper meeting the next, someone at a party might be standing with his or her back to you and later on turn round. There are almost unlimited variations possible and they are worth considering since the first impression a person makes upon you is often very significant, whether it is reinforced upon closer acquaintance or whether your impression changes as you come to know the stranger better.

We should also note that Lawrence suggests something of the man's personality in the dialogue even before he is seen: his voice is 'soft, softly-vibrating', 'melodious', 'rather scared', and his questions are simple, straightforward and he makes evident the reason for his presence quite quickly. He does not seem dangerous or devious despite the obvious uncertainty of the girls. It is a good example of a personality being suggested in slight, deft touches of description before we have even seen him properly. You should try, in your writing, not to miss an opportunity for including such clues to a character's being in the very first glimpse.

The relationship in this passage between the general impression of the man and the more detailed description of the more relevant aspects of his appearance is a third point to notice. At first, he is physically described in a general sense as 'a young soldier, with his heavy kit on his back'. That phrase puts him into a context and renders unnecessary any further detailed description of his dress: we are immediately able to see him in perspective as a soldier on leave or demobilised. He is, therefore, neatly 'placed'. A little later, Lawrence goes beyond this almost casual reference to dress and background and describes the man's face — 'a ruddy, roundish face, with fairish hair, rather long' — but that too is rather general description. The focus is directed towards a quality of his manner and being, which is seen in his eyes — we are twice told that they are bright, and they are sharp and he stares keenly — and which is also seen in his 'slightly glistening look', partly caused by the sweat that flattens his hair down to his forehead and partly by the appearance of the fine, fair hairs on his cheeks. In every way, he seems enquiring, sharp and perceptive, watching things keenly, and this impression is heightened by his having to thrust his head forward because of the heavy kit-bag he carries. Lawrence has picked out one quality and emphasised it through his detailed description. As a result, we have a strong, specific and coherent impression of this character and there is no sense of irrelevant detail merely padding out the portrait.

A further, and important, aspect of this description concerns the other characters present at this point when the youth enters the story. The description of his appearance is given all the time in terms of the effect he has on the two girls. March notices his 'strange, soft, modulated voice' which in some way influences her and, when she sees him, her reaction is quite strong: she stares at him 'spellbound' and does not move away. There is something mysterious and unexplained about this reaction, something that intrigues the reader and prompts interest in how they will relate together in the future. March's reaction, moreover, contrasts with that of Banford, who, being frightened, clings to her chair and only half looks at him. But, as well as describing the girls' reactions, Lawrence also enables us to see the youth as they saw him. The quality that he emphasises, which I discussed in the previous paragraph, is the quality that the girls themselves perceived. It is not irrelevant to mention again here that the title of the story is 'The Fox' and that, later on in the narrative, we become aware that this young stranger is to be identified with a fox: he is found to have the innate cunning and persistence of the animal. It is not, I think, too fanciful to suggest that the fox is present in this description as an implied comparison with the appearance of the stranger. That unstated comparison enables Lawrence to convey a coherence in the impression the man makes that might not otherwise have been present.

You will already, if you have read my commentary on this passage carefully, have started to think about ways in which you could apply some of the techniques that Lawrence uses in your own writing. A useful exercise would be to think of someone that you know well and, recalling in careful detail the time when you first met him, to write a couple of paragraphs describing that occasion. Try to include one or more of the following suggestions:

1. Introduce the character dramatically. Let him appear upon the scene by gradual stages.

2. Let the very first detail about him convey something of his character as the young man's voice does in the passage above.

3. Concentrate on some particular aspect of your subject's personality and let all your detailed description express that aspect. Avoid a catalogue of descriptive detail and give only a brief general impression as a background to the quality upon which you are going to focus.

4. Refer to the reactions of other people present or to your own reactions and perhaps include some dialogue. Lawrence implied a comparison between the youth and a fox; it may be that you can use a similar comparison, either stating openly what the character reminded you of on your first meeting, or, more subtly, implying a comparison in the way you describe him or her.

It will be an interesting comparison for us to look at one other short passage which contains a detailed description of a character's external appearance and concerns itself with the reaction of a known character to one who is appearing for the first time. The stranger is clearly, visually present to us but, in this passage, we are far more interested in what the character we already know feels about him. The extract is taken from the opening pages of Thomas Mann's short novel *Death in Venice*, and it describes how the hero, Aschenbach, sees a man standing in the portico of a building in Munich at the top of a flight of steps leading up to the doors.

He was of medium height, thin, beardless, and strikingly snub-nosed; he belonged to the red-haired type and possessed its milky, freckled skin. He was obviously not Bavarian; |and the broad, straight-brimmed straw hat he had
5 on even made him look distinctly exotic. True, he had the indigenous rucksack buckled on his back, wore a belted suit of yellowish woollen stuff, apparently frieze, and carried a grey mackintosh cape across his left forearm, which was propped against his waist. In his right hand, slantwise to the ground,
10 he held an iron-shod stick, and braced himself against its crook, with his legs crossed. His chin was up, so that the Adam's apple looked very bald in the lean neck rising from the loose shirt; and he stood there sharply peering up into

space out of colourless, red-lashed eyes, while two pro-
15 · nounced perpendicular furrows showed on his forehead in
curious contrast to his little turned-up nose. Perhaps his
heightened and heightening position helped out the impression Aschenbach received. At any rate, standing there as
though at survey, the man had a bold and domineering, even a
20 ruthless, air, and his lips completed the picture by seeming to
curl back, either by reason of some deformity or else because
he grimaced, being blinded by the sun in his face; they laid
bare the long, white, glistening teeth to the gums.

It is worthwhile noting the order in which Mann presents different
sorts of descriptive detail in this extract: it moves from the
generalised to the specific impression that his face creates in the
onlooker. At first, the stranger is categorised as being of a particular
physical type, red-haired and 'possessing its milky, freckled skin'.
Mann then relates him to the context of the country in which he is
clearly travelling. Although some aspects of his dress are
characteristic of Bavaria, he is obviously not Bavarian: he is of a
different physical type and his 'straight-brimmed straw hat' is
unusual to the point of being exotic. This raises a question mark
over his presence and produces a sense of uncertainty. In a familiar
place, someone very odd has appeared who is intriguing. The
reader's interest is aroused.

The author then elaborates a description of the stranger's dress
and, at the same time, he conveys exactly what stance the man has
assumed, standing cross-legged, leaning on a stick held in his right
hand and with his left hand on his hip. This gives him far more
reality of presence – we feel he is really there – than a bald
catalogue of his clothes, unrelated to the particular moment that is
being described.

The eyes of the onlooker, and therefore of the reader, move up to
notice the man's neck, with its Adam's apple, and then to the
striking features of the face. It is at this point that the 'air' of the
man, the impression that he creates in Aschenbach, is emphasised
and Mann incorporates the description of this bold, domineering
and ruthless air with the description of facial features. We see the
man and are aware of Aschenbach's feelings about him at the same
time. When the author has made clear the general impact of the
figure, which had, of course, been implied throughout the
description, the very manner of his stance being bold and

dominating, he leaves us with a clear image of the stranger's teeth, glistening and dangerous.

There follow some further suggestions for your own writing. Try to incorporate one or more of them in a composition involving the introduction of a stranger.

1. Introduce a character who is obviously strange to a place that you know well and whose appearance there mystifies the other people present. Arouse uncertainty about the stranger.

2. Follow a definite order in presenting a description of someone so that you gradually build up to some general but forceful impression created by the character. The passage above moves from definition of physical type to clothes and then to facial characteristics and the 'air' of the person, but there are many other ways of progressing.

3. Choose someone you have met or create a character who makes an immediate and very strong impact on your feelings and introduce him in a setting but static. The stranger in the extract from *Death in Venice* is standing still at the top of a flight of steps and this contributes to the effect of his personality. Visualise where your subject is standing, sitting or lying and let his posture contribute to the impact he makes on you.

Characters from within

We have looked at some ways of introducing characters through description of their external appearance and the effect they have on others and it is appropriate now to consider a rather different method of introducing a character, by narrating something of his own thoughts and feelings and observations. This is a way of writing which involves the author in getting inside the character he is creating and seeing the world through the character's eyes. The external descriptions we have examined might be more appropriate for the sort of composition topic that I quoted at the start of this chapter, but very often the candidate is invited to write a story or narrate events and a story can become far more fascinating if the events are seen from the viewpoint of one or more characters. If the character is presented strictly from within, without any comments from a narrator or other character, then the reader is able to know him rather more intimately; his personality is not being mediated to us through someone else's eyes but we are being invited into his innermost thoughts and feelings. There is an obvious similarity between this mode of constructing a novel and the sort of writing that is found in autobiographies, where the author reveals himself, his motives and tastes for our enjoyment and interest, and the type of composition question which invites the O-level candidate to write about his own experiences. As far as you are concerned, however, the difference between the two sorts of composition lies in the imaginative effort that is required if you decide to attempt to construct the processes of thinking and feeling and observing that go on inside a fictional character that you are creating.

As an example of the effect that may be achieved through writing from within a character, here is a passage taken from the start of a short story by Katherine Mansfield, called 'A Birthday'. It is from a collection of short stories entitled *In a German Pension*.

Andreas Binzer woke slowly. He turned over on the narrow bed and stretched himself – yawned – opening his mouth as widely as possible and bringing his teeth together afterwards with a sharp "click". The sound of that click fascinated him;
5   he repeated it quickly several times, with a snapping movement of the jaws. What teeth! he thought. Sound as a bell, every man jack of them. Never had one out, never had one stopped. That comes of no tomfoolery in eating, and a good regular brushing night and morning. He raised himself
10 on his left elbow and waved his right arm over the side of the bed to feel for the chair where he put his watch and chain overnight. No chair was there – of course, he'd forgotten, there wasn't a chair in this wretched spare room. Had to put the confounded thing under his pillow. "Half past eight,
15 Sunday, breakfast at nine – time for the bath" – his brain ticked to the watch. He sprang out of the bed and went over to the window. The Venetian blind was broken, hung fan-shaped over the upper pane ... "That blind must be mended. I'll get the office boy to drop in and fix it on his way
20 home tomorrow – he's a good hand at blinds. Give him twopence and he'll do it as well as a carpenter ... Anna could do it herself if she was all right. So would I, for the matter of that, but I don't like to trust myself on rickety step-ladders." He looked up at the sky: it shone, strangely white, unflecked
25 with cloud; he looked down at the row of garden strips and back yards. The fence of these gardens was built along the edge of a gully, spanned by an iron suspension bridge, and the

people had a wretched habit of throwing their empty tins over the fence into the gully. Just like them, of course! Andreas
30 started counting the tins, and decided, viciously, to write a letter to the papers about it and sign it — sign it in full.

The servant girl came out of their back door into the yard, carrying his boots. She threw one down on the ground, thrust
35 her hand into the other, and stared at it sucking in her cheeks. Suddenly she bent forward, spat on the toecap, and started polishing with a brush rooted out of her apron pocket ... "Slut of a girl! Heaven knows what infectious disease may be breeding now in that boot. Anna must get rid of that girl —
40 even if she has to do without one for a bit — as soon as she's up and about again. The way she chucked one boot down and then spat upon the other ! She didn't care whose boots she'd got hold of. *She* had no false notions of the respect due to the master of the house." He turned away from the window and
45 switched his bath towel from the wash-stand rail, sick at heart. "I'm too sensitive for a man — that's what's the matter with me. Have been from the beginning, and will be to the end."

Andreas Binzer comes alive for us although there is no external, physical description of the man in this passage at all. There is movement, the character rousing himself and getting out of bed, and a firm sense of the circumstances as we notice the things inside the room and seen through the window that he is aware of. We see the world through his eyes and we share the sequence of thoughts and observations that come to him. Very swiftly we come to realise the sort of person he is since Katherine Mansfield ensures that each detail indicates a characteristic attitude or preoccupation of the man.

Binzer snaps his teeth together and the action reminds him what a fine set he possesses. Full of self-admiration and self-regard, he clearly has a fine opinion of himself and of his way of life. He reveals his preoccupation with an orderly, routined existence in the reference to regular brushing and in his expectation of the chair beside his bed: he is one who gives way to irritation when things are not just as he thinks they should be. The broken Venetian blind likewise offends his idea of what is proper and his ideas about mending it reveals not only his meanness — we would expect that in a man so dependent on narrow routine, a small-minded man whose 'brain ticked to the watch' — but also shows the care he extends to himself: '"I don't like to trust myself on rickety stepladders."' He is censorious and unaccommodating of other people's failings in his, perhaps justifiable, dislike of those who threw their empty tins into the gully and, more clearly so, in his condemnation of the servant girl. His sense of his own importance is boundless as he contemplates the effect of his full signature on a letter of complaint and in the characteristic phrase, 'the respect due to the master of the house'. Meticulous and petty, his wrath is fully aroused by the sight of the servant girl spitting on his boots before polishing them.

What is rather more disturbing than these not unusual foibles is his immense selfishness, which only fully emerges later on in the story when we realise that, at this very moment, his wife is in labour expecting their first child. To satisfy his own finickity dislike of the servant, he is prepared to allow his wife, newly risen from her child-bed to do without a servant. He has no regard for the needs or feelings of others and it has not even crossed his mind to wonder how his wife is. What he views as being 'sensitive' in the last sentence is pure selfishness.

It is also worth noting that the passage is quite amusing. Binzer is a silly, pompous, selfish little man, demanding such high standards from other people that he is bound to be constantly frustrated and irritated. It is, of course, amusing to watch an ungenerous character reacting mechanically in a way that we can swiftly begin to anticipate.

If you have not already attempted to describe a character from within, you could make a start by following this procedure:

1. Determine clearly the sort of personality that your subject is. Does he think freely or within narrow, constricted limits? Does he feel strong emotions, of joy or anger or compassion or irritation, etc.? Does he rationalise his feelings, justify himself or simply respond to life without too much thought?

2. Decide whether or not you like your subject and how you are going to convey this estimate of him to your reader. Katherine Mansfield does not tell us directly what she thinks about Binzer but implicit in the detail of the passage is her feeling that he is a thorough male chauvinist pig!

3. Have a clear idea of exactly where your subject is and what he is doing. Binzer's actions and immediate circumstances provoke his thoughts and feelings, which, in turn, carry us into an understanding of his personality. Put your subject in a definite setting.

Characters interacting

It is perhaps false to discuss qualities of personality as if these were fixed and final things that never vary. It is true that everyone does have an identity, a personality which other people regard as more or less constant, but within that identity there is a great deal of movement, change and development within us. The people we meet affect us in different ways so that we have not exactly the same manner with this friend as with that one. Our moods and emotional states are determined by the experiences we have had and by the circumstances and people that are around us at any one time. They call forth particular reactions from us according to the personalities they themselves are.

Compare the way you function with people you know well with the way you function in a strange, unfamiliar setting. Certain groups of people will make you feel at ease and others will provoke feelings of shyness or of a need to assert yourself. All these movements and changes need to be taken into account when your writing involves two or more people who are interacting together. It is important that a description of people involved together in some activity or relating to each other should convey to the reader a sense of dynamic, of living response to experiences.

Some of the passages in the earlier chapter, 'Understanding People in Books', demonstrate the complex ways in which people affect each other and how the same circumstance may have subtly different effects on the various people involved. The two passages at the end of that chapter describing lovers together are both good examples of characters dynamically interacting. Miriam's feelings for Paul are intense enough to produce a conflict in him, which he can cope with only by getting away from her. The actions and moods of Vinca, in the passage from *Ripening Seed*, produces, at each point, a corresponding and different reaction from Phillipe.

In the final section of this chapter, I shall examine some situations from novels in which two or more people are in different ways relating to each other. This will help you to appreciate some of the possibilities for conveying the dynamic of personal interaction in your own writing. It is important that you should develop a sensitivity to the effect that characters you create – in a piece of narrative or description of an event or human situation – may have on each other. This sense of personal relationships, being established, growing and changing, will not only give a life-like quality to your writing, it will also help you to reveal your characters to the reader. As I have already implied, we do not **know** people as static, finished objects. We know them in action, in movement, in the way they do things and the way they say things. Your reader will come to know your characters all the better if they are seen to be alive, doing and speaking, their actions and words being partly determined by their own personalities and partly by the other people and circumstances around them.

First meeting

An obvious departure point for a discussion of interaction between characters is the description of two people meeting for the first time. What takes place on that occasion will depend on a number of factors to do with the personalities and previous experiences of the characters and the circumstances of meeting. These various factors might be separated out into the following questions:

1. What personalities do your two characters possess? What manner is each likely to assume when meeting someone for the first time? Is one of them shy and retiring and the other more self-confident, are they both easy in manner or both unwilling to make contact?

2. Do these two characters come from similar backgrounds and are they able to fit each other into a known context? For example, an older professional man, who had once spent a number of years working on a factory floor, might find it quite easy to relate to young factory-hand and see him as a person, whilst the young man would see the other simply as a stereotyped 'professional man', one of the bosses, and be unable or unwilling to feel easy with him. Our past experience often determines the way we react to people; you might find it easier to talk to a new pupil at school or college than you would to a tramp. The way that we talk to people is also often determined by the role we feel we should play in relation to others; for example, a boy in school, spoken to by his headmaster, would be

likely to assume a certain manner and this manner might well be very different from the one he would assume in talking to a stranger on the train, although, let us assume, that unknown to the boy this stranger was a headmaster.

3. What impact do the circumstances of meeting have on the people concerned? At a party, it is anticipated that people will make an effort to talk to each other, whereas you would not feel obliged to smile and chat to everyone at a disco. People do not normally talk to each other on the London tubes, whereas on a long coach journey, they would be much more likely at least to exchange a few words with the people sitting next to them.

Read the following passage with these questions in mind. It is the first few paragraphs of a novel by Joyce Cary, called *Mister Johnson*.

The young women of Fada, in Nigeria, are well known for beauty. They have small, neat features and their backs are not too hollow.

5   One day at the ferry over Fada River, a young clerk called Johnson came to take passage. The ferryman's daughter, Bamu, was a local beauty, with skin as pale and glistening as milk chocolate, high, firm breasts, round, strong arms. She could throw a twenty-foot pole with that perfect grace which 10 was necessary to the act, if the pole was not to throw her. Johnson sat admiring her with a grin of pleasure and called out compliments, "What a pretty girl you are."

Bamu said nothing. She saw that Johnson was a stranger. 15 Strangers are still rare in Fada bush and they are received with doubt. This is not surprising, because in Fada history all strangers have brought trouble; war, disease, or bad magic. Johnson is not only a stranger by accent, but by colour. He is as black as a stove, almost a pure Negro, with short nose and 20 full, soft lips. He is young, perhaps seventeen, and seems half-grown. His neck, legs, and arms are much too long and thin for his small body, as narrow as a skinned rabbit's. He is loose-jointed like a boy, and sits with his knees up to his nose, grinning at Bamu over the stretched white cotton of his

25   trousers. He smiles with the delighted expression of a child
      looking at a birthday table and says, "Oh, you are too pretty –
      a beautiful girl."

      Bamu pays no attention. She throws the pole, places the top
30   between her breasts against her crossed palms, and walks
      down the narrow craft.

      "What pretty breasts – God bless you with them."

35   Bamu recovers the pole and goes back for another throw.
      When Johnson lands, he walks backwards up the bank,
      laughing at her. But she does not even look at him.

There is not a great deal of interaction between these two
characters but what there is clearly demonstrates the relevance of
the questions I outlined above. Bamu is apparently shy and
unwilling to speak to a stranger at all, especially one who makes
such obvious advances to her. Her silence may, to some extent, be
the result of her personality but it is also very largely caused, as
Cary tells us, by her background. She belongs to a tribe in Nigeria
that has a deeply-rooted distrust of strangers, because they have
always brought ill-luck and damage to the life of the Fada people in
the past.

Johnson, on the other hand, is not governed by any inhibitions
caused by convention. He seems very out-going, rather naïve, and
totally unaware that he makes himself slightly ridiculous. He is not
at all perturbed by the complete indifference with which Bamu
greets his approaches to her. Nor is he the least bit subtle in stating
precisely what he feels.

We cannot be absolutely certain how the circumstances have
affected this meeting. Johnson is travelling, apparently rootless,
and perhaps feels far more free. Bamu has a job to do and is able
to concentrate on going through the actions of ferrying him
across the river without paying any apparent attention to what he
is saying. The meeting is, however, perfectly 'placed', description
of the situation interwoven with description of the actions and
appearance of the two characters, so that, in spite of the place
being rather far from the experience of most of us, the situation
comes alive; it seems a small and intriguing piece of genuine
human experience.

It will not be difficult for you to create a few paragraphs describing an encounter between two strangers. Choose a definite situation and visualise it clearly in your mind before writing so that you can incorporate a few descriptive details, either presenting them as narrator or letting your characters notice them in the course of the meeting. Then, determine the personalities and manner of your characters; it will be easier for you to distinguish them and convey their personalities if one feels more at ease in this situation than the other. I would suggest that you make this an exercise in constructing dialogue, thinking, at each point, of what the characters would be likely to say to each other, given their different personalities and feelings about the situation. You will find a brief summary of the rules involved in writing accurate dialogue on page 195. Be careful that you punctuate correctly.

Here are a few precise situations that you may care to develop:

1. A nervous boy approaches a girl who is chatting with her friends at a disco or party and asks for a dance.

2. A tramp engages someone in conversation in order eventually to ask for money. The other person is a little nervous but feels he or she should react politely.

3. A cheerful, friendly character tries to cheer up a withdrawn visitor, who is obviously feeling ill-at-ease and miserable.

4. A salesman with tact and persistence is able to talk round a self-opinionated woman into buying something.

Feelings: self-abandonment or control?

A first encounter between two people limits the range of interaction between people to what is usually fairly simple and easy to cope with in your writing, but you are likely in your compositions to want and to need to develop the way your characters interact beyond this manageable starting point, however fascinating that first encounter in itself may be. If you were going to tackle the second of the two questions I quoted at the start of this chapter – the one that asks you to write about your impressions of your form and its characters – you would be dealing with people that you know very well and have seen under a considerable variety of circumstances. You would need to recreate some incidents which will give the reader an experience of your chosen

PRAISE FOR 'EXAMINER-PLAN' COURSES FROM EXAMINERS AND STUDENTS

EXAMINERS WRITE: 'In my opinion there is no doubt about the 'Examiner-Plan' being the best way to prepare for GCE Examinations at home' ▪ 'All they (the students) could ever need for distinction or Grade 'A'' ▪ 'Students are getting very good value here — may I wish the courses every blessing' ▪ 'Excellent scheme — good luck' ▪ 'The course (Maths) is logical and concise, yet has left out no important steps' ▪ 'The lessons explain in full detail all the methods, techniques and processes which you require to know' ▪ 'As a teacher who has prepared hundreds of students for their 'O'-level examinations over a period of twenty years, and as an examiner who has marked Home and Overseas GCE papers for much of that time, I am sure that any student following these 'Examiner-Plan' courses will have an excellent prospect of success in his chosen subjects'.

STUDENTS WRITE: **Maths. Ordered Course in Oct. — Grade 'C' in June (8 months).** 'Thank you for the valuable assistance received from your Course for Maths. Syl. D. I took the examination in June and received the result, Grade 'C', that I desired.'

Geography — Wonderful Success (3 months). 'Having had wonderful success with your 'O' Level Geography in June, my daughter would like details of the Maths Course.'

History — Started Nov. Passed with 'B' Grade June (7 months) 'Took 'O'-level History in June — am pleased to tell you that I passed obtaining a Grade 'B'. As you can imagine I am very satisfied with the result. I found the Course most instructive and enjoyable.' (now enrolled for Geography).

Grade 'B' in English After 6 months. 'I am delighted to report a first time pass at Grade 'B' (English Language). I commenced in December and completed just before the examination in early June — 6 months all told. This is the first examination I have ever sat and is a tremendous booster in my abilities.'

SEND FOR THE 'EXAMINER-PLAN' BROCHURE TODAY

characters in action, responding to each other and to whatever has provoked the particular incident.

It will be particularly helpful for you to have developed some skills in conveying the infinite variety of reactions that may take place amongst people who know each other well when you come to write about your own family. Almost every exam. paper set by any of the boards contains a question inviting you to write about some incident or situation that has taken place within the family setting or to write about the characters of your parents or other relations. There are also frequent questions on the 'generation gap' which, though primarily asking for your views on various aspects of the ways older people treat younger people, could easily lead to narrate one or two illustrative incidents.

When you think about the way members of your class or family relate together and of the various situations that spring into your mind, you will immediately be aware of seemingly endless possibilities for different reactions between the characters present and for an overall mood or 'atmosphere'. People may be happy, sad, irritable, cheerful, etc. for different reasons and in different degrees and these may contribute to the generally prevailing mood of the group in all sorts of different ways. A minor accident may occur in a cheerful group of people and it will set off slightly different reactions in everyone present but it may not upset the mood of the group. The same accident occuring at another time, when people are feeling tense or tired, may well produce an outburst of irritation which will be communicated throughout the group and lead to squabblings or a major row.

To help you be aware of these complex interactions in your own writing about people, I am going to set two passages against each other which demonstrate the extreme ways in which people may deal with their feelings. In the first extract, from a short story by James Joyce, taken from his collection of short stories, *Dubliners*, a man abandons himself completely to anger. The feeling takes him over so that he reacts with intense irritation and violence to things which, in normal circumstances, would probably have had little effect upon him. The story is called 'Counterparts'.

A very sullen-faced man stood at the corner of O'Connell Bridge waiting for the little Sandymount tram to take him home. He was full of smouldering anger and revengefulness.

He felt humiliated and discontented; he did not even feel
drunk; and he had only twopence in his pocket. He cursed
everything. He had done for himself in the office, pawned his
watch, spent all his money; and he had not even got drunk.
He began to feel thirsty again and he longed to be back in the
hot, reeking public-house. He had lost his reputation as a
strong man, having been defeated twice by a mere boy. His
heart swelled with fury and, when he thought of the woman
in the big hat who had brushed against him and said
"*Pardon!*" his fury nearly choked him.

His tram let him down at Shelbourn Road and he steered his
great body along in the shadow of the wall of that barracks.
He loathed returning to his home. When he went in by the
side-door he found the kitchen empty and the kitchen fire
nearly out. He bawled upstairs:

"Ada! Ada!"

His wife was a little sharp-faced woman who bullied her
husband when he was sober and was bullied by him when he
was drunk. They had five children. A little boy came running
down the stairs.

"Who is that?" said the man, peering through the darkness.

"Me, pa."

"Who are you? Charlie?"

"No, pa. Tom."

"Where's your mother?"

"She's out at the chapel."

"That's right... Did she think of leaving any dinner for me?"

"Yes, pa. I—"

"Light the lamp. What do you mean by having the place in
darkness? Are the other children in bed?"

The man sat down heavily on one of the chairs while the little

boy lit the lamp. He began to mimic his son's flat accent, saying half to himself: "*At the chapel. At the chapel, if you*
50 *please!*" When the lamp was lit he banged his fist on the table and shouted:

"Where's my dinner?"

55 "I'm going . . . to cook it, pa," said the little boy.

The man jumped up furiously and pointed to the fire.

"On that fire! You let the fire out! By God, I'll teach you to do
60 that again!"

He took a step to the door and seized the walking-stick which was standing behind it.

What will happen now is a foregone conclusion; in fact, it has been inevitable ever since the moment when the little boy came running down the stairs. Given the man's whole-hearted abandonment of himself to his anger, he was bound to take out his anger on the boy in some way. What is so skilful in this writing is the way Joyce piles detail upon detail, gradually feeding the fire of the man's anger until it must burst out in an explosion. We feel a tension as we read, wondering when the outburst will occur and what will be the consequences. The timing, the build-up of tension in the reader, is clearly of vital importance in this passage, as is the entirely convincing sequence of frustrations that the man suffers. A man in the grip of a passionate feeling of any sort will look for a means of getting rid of his intense feelings. His mind smoulders over the things that have happened to him and he becomes furious at thinking of a woman who had brushed against him in a perfectly ordinary way. He is trying to bring his anger to a crisis point and to thereby diminish it but angry thoughts only add fuel to his frustration.

All our actions, throughout our lives, are governed by the interplay between our thoughts and our feelings. At times, feelings are uppermost and we will not think before acting and, in many situations, this will be healthy and natural. At other times, we may have a clear idea of what we want to do or ought to do and we will decide not to allow strong feelings to gain ground within us, in case they come between us and the course of action we have decided upon. Our decision, which may not be a conscious one, as to whether or not we will be governed, at any particular moment, by our thoughts or our feelings will greatly affect our relationships with others. I daresay this may seem very obvious to you and rather general but you will find it helpful if you are uncertain about how you are going to develop your characters' reactions to each other at any particular point in your narrative to ask yourself the question: 'Is this character going to be carried away by the feelings that these people or this situation have caused in him or is he going to decide not to act upon impulse?'

Another way of asking what is virtually the same question is to say, 'Is this situation one in which the characters are acting spontaneously, without too much careful direction of themselves, or is it a situation in which the persons involved are controlling their reactions to each other?' The following passage provides us with an example of people manoeuvring around each other, not reacting with direct feelings but relating to each other as if it were a game of chess that was being played. It is taken from *A Girl in Winter* by Philip Larkin and it begins with a Chief Librarian telling off one of his assistants for some minor error that she has committed. I have abridged the extract slightly.

"But if, as I am saying or rather suggesting to you, you should in the fullness of time achieve a position comparable to mine, you will find that three-quarters of your time is taken up by looking out for and clearing up after some crackheaded girl
5 who thinks she's wrapped up a book and sent it to Wigan or Timbuctoo, when all she's actually done is to put it on the shelves where it ought n't to be." He laughed again, and pulled at his pipe, surrounding his head with blue, sweetish smoke.
10
Katherine looked at him as if he were an insect she would relish treading on. "I apologise for the mistake," she said furiously, "but I don't think that —"
15 "Well, well, Miss Lind, that's how we have to spend our time," Mr Anstey interrupted half-way through what she had said. He sat in an ugly position and slapped his thigh ruefully, grinning at her with his face distorted sideways. "Worrying about fiddling little details that won't matter in six weeks to

20 you or me or anyone else, while the really important things go
hang." . . .

There was a tap on the door, and Miss Feather entered,
glancing around as if she suspected there were more than two
25 people in the room. Mr Anstey at once put on his distant
expression, saying in a preoccupied voice:

"Yes, what is it, Miss Feather?"

30 "I'm afraid one of the juniors is feeling badly, Mr Anstey. She
isn't fit for work."

"And who is it, Miss Feather?" This was a third manner, that
of the judiciary alert to learn all the facts of the case.

35 "Miss Green. She really looks very ill."

"What's the matter with her?" he demanded harshly. "Is
she sickening for something, influenza or measles or—"

40 "She has very bad toothache, and she wants to go home. I
think it would be as well to let her. She won't be much use
here, really."

45 "Go home! It's a dentist she ought to go to," said Mr Anstey
contemptuously, as if detecting a subterfuge.

"I think she will, if we let her go home first." Miss Feather,
perhaps alone on the staff, had the knack of keeping Mr
50 Anstey fairly close to the point: she inserted submissive,
insinuating remarks that urged him gently back to the path
she wished him to follow.

"Where does she live? Is her mother on the telephone?" He
55 picked up the directory, disregarding Miss Feather's denial,
and discovered she was not.

"It's quite a long way," said Miss Feather. "I wonder if it
wouldn't be better to send someone with her. She seems
60 almost likely to faint."

"Why not give a holiday all round?" agreed Mr Anstey, with

a crowing, hysterical laugh. "I'll go with her myself if it means getting the morning off!"

65

He laughed alone.

"I think the best thing would be to send someone with her," repeated Miss Feather, glancing furtively at the clock on the
70 mantelpiece. Mr Anstey, chuckling good-humouredly, stuck his pipe back into his mouth and turned again to his papers.

"Yes, all right, all right," he said with indulgent impatience, as if they had both been wasting his time. "Send someone
75 with her. I don't mind who. Send someone—ha, ha!—you'd be glad to get rid of for an hour or two."

They left him enclosed in his unbreakable belief that all things depended on him, and that he managed, despite an
80 overwhelming weight of work, to administer every detail efficiently.

Mr Anstey is clearly a very unpleasant and odious character, the sort of person who does everything for effect and needs constantly to bolster up his own ego by dominating and manipulating other people. At the start of this extract, we hear him praising his own achievements, which are, in fact, quite modest, and utterly disregarding the feelings of Katherine Lind. She has made a very minor mistake but he uses this opportunity to utter a string of pretentious and unnecessary sentiments, some of which are not included in the extract printed above. Katherine's anger grows within her but, because of her subordinate position, she is unable to openly express her anger. Instead of saying what she really feels, she starts with, 'I apologize for the mistake.' Perhaps, at this moment, Anstey realises how angry she is and, unwilling to confront her strong feelings, with which he might not easily be able to deal, he cuts her short, not allowing her to utter the criticism of him which is on the tip of her tongue.

So, at the opening of this passage, we see Anstey posing as the self-righteous, efficient and hard-working man, whose time is being wasted by some stupid girl and Katherine forced to play the part of the stupid girl who has no right to speak out in self-defence.

When Miss Feather enters, Anstey assumes a sequence of assumed

134

poses – the distant, preoccupied man, the intent judge seeking for facts, and, finally, the good-humoured boss who can patronisingly cope with his subordinates' weaknesses – all designed to maintain his sense of superiority over his subordinates. His only way of communicating with his subordinates is through these assumed roles. But Miss Feather, to our considerable satisfaction, out-manoeuvres him. As Larkin says, she has the knack of steering him into doing what she wants him to do and she does this by giving him the means of acting as she suggests without in any way disturbing his sense of self-importance. Notice, for example, the clever way in which she glances 'furtively at the clock on the mantelpiece'. She must have meant the gesture to have been noticed by Mr Anstey, who promptly takes up the cue that he can reasonably appear to be an extremely busy person, to whom every minute matters. Miss Feather may well be acting on instinct rather than by conscious manoeuvres but she is effective all the same.

You are unlikely to have experienced exactly this situation but there must have been times when you or people around you have taken on a manner in order to create a particular effect on others. There are times when all of us want to cause something to happen involving others and use every means to bring them round to acting as we wish. Moreover, the complex society in which we live constantly forces us to assume roles in relation to other people. As I mentioned before, there is an implied manner of relating to a headmaster in his own school, which might not apply elsewhere. A teacher might tend to assume a different manner when he is at work from the one that would come naturally with a young friend of his family.

Taken together, the passage from *Dubliners* and the one from *A Girl in Winter* provide two extreme examples of very different modes of human interaction. In the former, feelings are fully expressed and issue in actions; in the latter, feelings are suppressed in order that the characters may more effectively pursue their aims. It is all the difference between a random game of soccer in which little attention is paid to the rules of the game and a painstakingly careful game of chess.

I am going to suggest two situations, both related to family life, for you to write about. You may well be able to think of many more.

1. Imagine that a boy or girl has been out for the evening and, for a variety of reasons, has returned home rather later than had been

agreed previously with his or her parents. The parents have, themselves, had a long and tiring day and, as the evening wore on, became irritable. The late return of their son or daughter is the last straw and either one or both of them show signs of exploding into anger. Let the anger simmer for a while before the row breaks. The boy or girl may have also had a rather unsatisfactory evening and, under pressure of the parents' irritation, eventually loses the capacity for tact. Remember to give the situation a setting; a few descriptive details that catch the eyes of the characters or a few movements involving reference to objects or furniture in the room would be enough to enable your reader to sense that this event is happening somewhere and not in thin air. Remember, also, to develop a clear sense of the different characters. It is unlikely that both the parents will express their irritation or anger in precisely the same way.

2. An alternative situation in which feelings are controlled and a certain amount of manoeuvring between people goes on might occur when a young person wishes to escape from a family gathering and go off for the evening. The parents have invited visitors and want the whole family to be at home. Because visitors are present, a row does not emerge when the son or daughter makes a bid to escape what promises to be a thoroughly tedious evening. Describe the conversation that occurs and the way different people react. Resolve the situation in whatever way seems appropriate to the characters.

To round off this chapter, let us consider the various suggestions I have been making about ways of describing characters and relate them to some composition questions that have been set in recent years.

Describe two of your friends who have contrasting qualities.
The essay might begin with a fairly brief description of how you met one of these friends. This could be done dramatically and contain details of external appearance and manner that would all convey something of the friend's character (look back to the passage from *The Fox*, page 114). The character could speak for itself without your supplying a list of qualities. The essay might then proceed by introducing the second friend and, rather than describe again a first meeting, you could concentrate on the way you habitually react to him, the impression he makes on you, or you could describe an incident which reveals his personality,

something which has happened with friends or his family. You could then go on to briefly summarise the differences you perceive between these two people and imagine how each would react under different sets of circumstances. Consider whether they are the sort of people who easily give way to their feelings or tend to control them.

The last day of your holiday at a seaside resort.

If you look back to the section called 'Characters from within', page 120, you will realise that a number of the suggestions that were drawn from the passage by Katherine Mansfield might be applied equally well to conveying the experience of such a day. The things you saw, heard, etc., your feelings and moods and reactions to various incidents must, in the course of the essay, give the reader a sense of your own personality. The reader will want to experience the place and the events of the day through your eyes.

Preparing for a party.

This would constitute a good opportunity for displaying the characters of various friends as, in different ways, they show their excitement or nervousness as they prepare the food and room. If there is an accident – someone tips a dish of peanuts all over the floor – how do people react?

Write a description or a story suggested by the accompanying picture.

The picture on the previous page shows a young man looking back at a girl he has just walked past on the road. It appears to be a lonely spot and she is carrying a heavy case. She is looking at a sign-post in some bewilderment. You have a perfect invitation to develop a description of a first encounter between two strangers. Decide what personalities the characters have and who is likely to feel most at ease and do most of the talking. Describe how each sees the other and what each feels about the other.

Chapter 7
Narrating Events

In the last two chapters, we have been considering some of the fundamental skills of good imaginative writing and, in this chapter, we shall be looking at the ways in which these skills may be applied in treating a sequence of events. We shall be taking a rather wider view, looking at the effect of a composition or short story as a whole rather than concentrating on detailed development of sections of an essay. I have already emphasised that you should develop a personal response to any place or situation you are describing and that you should choose and control details describing people, things or places so that there is nothing irrelevant in your writing. It is important that you maintain this ideal of a clear but rich and personal vision of your material when you come to write about a sequence of events, either to construct a short story or to recapture some incident from your past experience.

When describing events, a balance has to be maintained. On the one hand, the descriptive detail must not overwhelm the narration with the result that the sense of something actually happening is swamped by a mass of trivial or irrelevant detail. On the other hand, nothing is more unsatisfactory than a sequence of bald, unadorned events – 'Then we did this . . . Then we went to . . . After that we . . .' You need to make the effort of imaginatively *realising* the situation the characters are in and including descriptive detail that gives a firm sense of the narration being rooted in place and time and the people being real people with their individual thoughts, feelings and taste.

You are almost certain to encounter the possibility of writing essays on two sorts of topics in the examination, both types of question involving the construction of a sequence of events. All the examination boards tend to invite candidates to write about their memories, to reminisce about happenings in the past and they also invariably provide an opportunity for the candidate to write a short story. Here are some examples of these topics. I have included them at the start of this chapter so that you may have some idea of the difficulties that we shall be considering in the course of the chapter. I suggest that you choose a couple of these topics and ponder in detail over how you would develop them before you read on through the rest of this chapter. Try to define clearly where any points of difficulty arise.

Questions involving personal reminiscence

1. Describe an occasion when you panicked.

2. Experiences of a Saturday job.

3. 'I was only trying to help.' Describe an incident from your own experience, in which this explanation — or one like it — was offered.

4. What incidents or experiences in your childhood seem to you to have been the most important in forming your personality and ideas?

5. Describe an occasion when you were troubled by a guilty conscience.

Short stories

1. Write a short story to illustrate one of the following sayings:
   (a) The best things in life are free
   (b) Don't count your chickens before they are hatched
   (c) If a thing's worth doing, it's worth doing well.

2. The missing child. Write a story involving the disappearance or loss of a child. You may write as a parent, guardian, searcher, or as the child.

3. The following is the beginning of a short story by H. G. Wells:

   "I must get rid of it," said the man in the corner of the carriage, abruptly breaking the silence.

   Mr Hinchcliff looked up, hearing imperfectly. He stared across the carriage at his fellow-traveller.

   "Why not give it away?" said this person. "Give it away! Why not?"

   He was a tall, dark sunburnt man with a pale face. His arms were folded tightly, and his feet were on the seat in front of him. He was pulling at a lank black moustache. He stared hard at his toes.

"Why not?" he said.

Mr Hinchcliff coughed.

Continue this story in a manner which seems to you to be appropriate and interesting, without copying out the passage printed above.

4. You will find two drawings on pages 142 and 143. Together they make up a 'before and after' sequence. Tell the story of this event from the point of view of one or more of the people involved.

'Realising' a memory

It seems to me that the first problem you are likely to encounter in dealing with a question which invites you to recreate a memory is recollecting a sequence of events which seems significant or unusual enough to warrant writing about. You may be able to call to mind an occasion when you panicked or were troubled by a guilty conscience but the events may not seem powerful enough in themselves to hold the reader's attention. There is a snare here. What makes a narration come alive is not just the order of things that happened but the way in which the narrative is told. The reader must be able to identify with you or other characters, to understand why people acted as they did, and so your feelings and reactions must seem true to life. The reader also needs to be able to grasp the situation clearly, so you must include some relevant descriptive detail suggesting the circumstances. You should not worry if your memories, real or imagined, do not seem particularly exciting. As long as you can fully *realise* the situation, which means a steady concentration on what is actually happening within and between the characters, the writing will be convincing.

However, as I mentioned at the start of this chapter, there are two pitfalls to be avoided: that of failing to fill out the narrative, providing merely a thin skeleton of happenings, and that of swamping the narrative with trivia or irrelevant details. The last two chapters give plenty of ideas for the enrichment of description. The dangers of over-writing or trivialising the

narration may be appreciated by comparing the following two extracts from essays written by fourteen-year-old pupils of a London school. The subject was 'My Experiences of Rush-hour in the Underground'.

A. It had been hot outside but as I stepped on to the escalator a cooling breeze reached my face and I was grateful for it. As I looked to the side of me, rather insignificant advertisements flashed by. To think that people actually pay for that space on
5 the wall and nobody an really take them in, because they go past so quickly – not that I think many people do want to take them in. Suddenly the end of the escalator loomed up in front of me and I stepped off. For the first time I became aware of all the people around me. I stopped and looked at the signs and
10 arrows to find out the right platform. People were pushing past me in all directions, all knowing exactly where to go except me. Suddenly an extra large crowd of people came jolting off the escalator and as the noise of the approaching train was heard they began to break into a run. I was literally
15 carried along with them and my only hope was that I was being pushed on to the right train. Before I could do anything, the doors closed shut and I was trapped. It certainly was like a tin of sardines. I didn't have to hold on to anything because I was supported by the people around me. The train had pulled
20 off and now we were in the tunnel. Down here I felt rather like a mole except that moles don't get other moles standing on their toes. I looked up straight into a newspaper. I tried to shift myself but his feet were still on top of mine. Suddenly the train slowed down and when the doors opened I gave my
25 foot a huge tug and it was free. Then more people pushed into our compartment and the squash was worse than before. I wondered how some people could suffer this endurance day after day, year after year. The only conclusion that I came to was that they must be mad. The train quickly rattled through
30 the tunnels and past stations.

B. I step down from the train. A dismal stench hangs in the air and fills the station with gloom. The sky is overcast and the ground is wet and muddy. I amble over to the stairs marked "UNDERGROUND". Suddenly a crowd of shuffling
5 bustling people surround me, all wanting to get on the Underground and all determined to be the first. They rush around me, carrying me downstairs with them. The noise of

144

the angry feet hitting the iron stairs echoes like a stampede of horses. I rush down the stairs, unavoidably rubbing shoulders and scraping elbows with my fellow travellers until I reach the bottom.

Then, like a snake in the grass, the direction of the horde changes as we all scamper along a passage-way leading to the ticket offices. Here the crowd spreads out to fill all the corners of the hall, some busily searching their baggage to find their money, some holding their tickets out in front of their noses as if they were the only ones in the world who had one, and others swirling their heads about to see that all the members of their party are present. Great queues congregated at the barriers. One person at a time is shunted through the barriers like a machine making chocolate, turning out its produce to a constant hum. Soon the great crowd of travellers was infesting the tunnels, all trying to overtake each other and hardly any of them succeeding.

Neither of these is disastrous and both would pass at ordinary level but there is a gossipy silliness about *A* which would not commend the piece to the examiner. This candidate's comments on the advertisements lining the escalator walls detract from a realisation of the scene. The reader has forced upon him some mediocre reflections which, rather than helping him to be more aware of the scene in the underground, tend to focus attention on the writer's assumption of a pert and superficial superiority. The attempt in this passage to be clever disguises the fact that the writer has not concentrated on conveying a realistic sense of the underground. 'An extra large crowd' does not 'suddenly' jolt off an escalator since you cannot stand more than two abreast on it. It is unlikely that a traveller will be unwillingly pushed on to a train, without being able to make sure that it is the right one; even in the height of the rush-hour, it is possible to stand aside and look at the station maps. People do not stand for long periods on other people's toes. In the unlikely event of such a thing happening, one would be a fool not to politely request release; 'I gave my foot a huge tug and it was free' does not strike the reader as a realistic occurrence. The candidate's comment on the sanity of the working populace of London is similarly unconvincing.

B has concentrated on recreating the scene rather than on including ill-considered and trivial comments. He suggests the atmosphere of the day in the first sentence and notices telling details, such as the noise of feet on iron stairs, and the different and characteristic movements of individuals in the crowded ticket-office. Some people do hold out their tickets 'as if they were the only ones in the world who had one' and there is a constant hum of people moving through the barriers. He manages to suggest quite deftly the ineffective competition of travellers trying to overtake each other in the tunnels. More could have been done with this situation and a lack of concentration is noticeable in the candidate's uncertainty over tenses – he lapses into the past in lines 20 and 23 – but, on the whole, this is a convincing piece of writing and there is little irrelevant detail.

So, in realising a memory or creating an imaginary one, remember that the more detail – of the scene, of people's reactions, of your own real feelings – that you can realise in your mind, the more likely you will be to write a well-conceived and convincing essay. Avoid trivialising your narration with irrelevance. Concentrate on the memory itself, not on self-display or the artificial creation of an effect.

Constructing a short story

Much that I have said about describing personal memories is relevant to the writing of short stories. The line between recreation of past events and developing an apparently fictional narrative, which may well be based partly or wholly on your experience, is a thin one, memories of real events and matter developed through imagination usually being combined in both types of writing. But, whether fictional or drawn from memory, your story must convince and it will be convincing if you conceive the characters clearly and allow their actions to issue naturally from their personalities. Descriptive detail suggesting the background and setting for the action will also help to create a sense of rich reality in the story line.

I suggested that you might encounter the hurdle of apparently insignificant or trivial events when dealing with personal memories, and a similar problem may well face you as you contemplate the task of writing a short story under examination conditions. What on earth is going to happen in this story? The possibilities may be bewildering and no one sequence of events may come clear enough in your mind for you to choose it as worthy of detailed treatment.

Consider the four topics suggested on pages 140 and 141. It seems to me that the fourth topic involving the two drawings is by far the easiest one to deal with if you are to start writing without too much hesitation. You are presented with a number of people in a situation, something quite dramatic occurs and the same people are present at the end of the story, only they are in quite different states of mind and they are now relating to each other with a different range of feelings. What you are required to do is merely to show what went on, both inside the individual characters and in the external world, which caused these people to move from situation *A* to situation *B*. Put in over-simplified terms, this is all that a short story is: conceive of a starting point and of a finishing point and show how your characters move from the one to the other.

Since the fourth topic provides you with opening and concluding situations, it is the easiest of these subjects to tackle. Furthermore, the intervening event is obvious and not complicated, so you are free to concentrate on the characters and on setting the scene within a fairly simple framework of action. The second topic, 'The missing child', is not quite so accessible, in that you have more freedom for deciding how the story will begin (the child, enjoying the pleasures of a fairground in company with older brothers or sisters, realises that he is lost . . ., a parent expects her young son, who is out playing with his friends, to come in to tea but he fails to arrive . . ., etc.) and you have a considerable range of possible endings from the tragic death of the child to the recognition that it was all a mistake and he was not lost at all. However, the possibilities are limited by the subject set and as long as you can decide fairly quickly how the story begins and how it will end you should not have too much difficulty in embarking on the narration.

The topics under question 1 demand rather more of the candidate, who must conceive of a whole sequence of events with very little initial guidance. My advice to you is to decide, before you think of anything else, exactly how the story is going to end. Get clear in your mind the situation that will conclude the story, the point at which the characters have arrived. It is helpful to think of this 'arrival' as involving one or more characters in some sort of recognition or realisation. For example, Mr X, who has spent all his life acquiring money and possessions, but for all that lives an isolated, loveless existence, encounters someone who is quite unimpressed by his wealth but likes him as a person. He glimpses the possibility of a different way of life. Or, Mr X finds himself accidentally stranded in a place where money is no use and he finds, to his surprise, that he is released into enjoying ordinary, simple pleasures, that 'the best things in life are free'. Someone who is naturally lazy and inefficient realises the truth of (c) either because his inefficiency causes disaster for himself or others or because he gets caught up in doing something well and enjoys a new sense of satisfaction. Whatever situation you choose, decide first on a conclusion, then take a starting point and work towards the climax.

Creating a satisfactory climax

It is important to remember that in the examination you have limited time available in which to write a short story. A complicated sequence of events is to be avoided at all costs or you will find yourself so preoccupied with what happened next that you will be unable to develop your characters at all or relate their actions to their personalities. Much can be achieved by conceiving clearly of one human situation and elaborating and intensifying the feelings of the people involved so that it reaches a crisis point. The crisis is likely to be most effective if it is simple and the result of a slightly unexpected twist in the action.

In this matter of building to a climax, you, as the writer, hold the trump card for you know how you intend to conclude your story whilst your reader cannot know this for certain and may be kept in suspense. This need not be difficult to achieve. In any human situation, there is an enormous range of possible developments. As you explore your characters and reveal more about them and the situation which is the initial point of departure for the story, the reader will begin to wonder how things will work out. He may experience a sense of impending disaster or resolution but he will not know exactly how that will occur. If you have managed to arouse his interest in one of your characters, then he will want to know that character's fate in the context of your story. Keep him waiting for a while.

Here is an example of one way of letting a situation simmer and then rise to a climax. The crisis comes as sudden activity bursting in on a scene of tension between people. Charles, an out-of-work ex-student, has called on Robert and Edith, who are his girl-friend's sister and brother-in-law. He is trying to find out where his girl-friend is but they will not help and instead start criticising him. I have abbreviated the extract (from *Hurry on Down*, by John Wain) slightly.

The voices of Robert and Edith splashed on and on. Charles tried to be oblivious of them, but the smug phrases, the pert half-truths, the bland brutalities, ripped down his defences. It was finally a remark of Edith's that brought him to his feet in
5   a sudden rush of anger.

"You never seem to want to repay any of the people who've tried to help you.". . .

10 On his feet, gripping the back of his chair, Charles sought for a quick, devastating reply: a few words so swift and bitter that they would scorch themselves into Edith's mind and live with her, waking and sleeping, till she died.

15 "Your shaft seems to have gone home, Edith," said her husband. "Our friend doesn't quite know how to answer you. It's reduced him to silence."

Charles focused with sudden clarity on Robert. All at once it
20 seemed to him that the stiff brown moustache which he wore to give dignity to his face was curiously non-human. It looked as if it had been clipped from the face of an Airedale.

"I wasn't really thinking about what Edith had said," he
25 replied half apologetically. "I was just wondering why no one's ever found it worth while to cut off that silly moustache of yours and use it for one of those brushes you see hanging out of windows next to the waste pipe."

30 He spoke quietly and courteously; nevertheless they realised, after a short pause in which their minds groped for the meaning of his words, that he was being definitely insulting.

Edith's face seemed to swell up to twice its size, her eyes
35 bulged and she began a loud and unsteady tirade, quavering with hysteria but heavy with menace. Robert, on the other hand, had no difficulty in selecting the basic attitude proper for him to adopt. His mouth tightened, he squared his shoulders, and he moved forward, lightly and yet
40 decisively . . . He grasped Charles by the lapel of his jacket. For an instant surprise gripped Charles and held him

149

motionless. How quickly, how fatally, the situation had developed! So now, finally, he had put himself in the wrong. "Quite abusive. In fact Robert had to put him out. Impossible
45 to have him in the house again."

Robert's pouchy, inane face was thrust aggressively into his. Hell! They could have it if they wanted it. With a sudden twist he broke free, lunged across to the sink and snatched up
50 the washing-up bowl. Edith had just finished washing up when he arrived, and for some reason she had not thrown the water away. Half of the scummy grey flood poured over Charles himself as he dragged the bowl wildly out of the sink, but the other half cascaded gloriously as, with a tremendous
55 sense of release, he swung it round. Almost simultaneously three sounds filled the kitchen – the water's gulping splash, Edith's loud squealing, and the clatter of the empty bowl landing in a corner. It had hardly landed before Charles clawed open the back door and rushed out. A backward
60 glance showed him Edith's face framed in wisps of wet hair, and Robert trying to blink the soap from his eyes.

Chapter 8
Writing about Your Tastes
or Personal Interests

In this chapter, I shall deal with a range of essay topics which would involve you, at some point in each of these essays, in writing about your likes and dislikes. Such subjects may take the form of an invitation or suggestion that the candidate write about hobbies or interests or the subject may be more general, suggesting that a reflective essay, including reminiscences and imaginary situations as well as statement of personal views or taste, would be appropriate. Here are some examples of the sort of essay topic I have in mind:

1. Describe the appeal of either membership of a minority group, or an unusual pastime.

2. What enjoyment do you derive from watching or listening to serial programmes?

3. 'We would all be idle if we could.' Discuss this statement.

4. The importance of music in your daily life.

5. 'I'd rather go by train than by car.'

6. Art in everyday life.

As you see from this fairly random selection of topics from recent papers, this type of essay subject is often presented very briefly, leaving the candidate to develop his essay as he wishes. Each one of these titles is an opportunity for the candidate to write an essay which is not concerned solely with describing people or describing places, not simply a narration of a sequence of events and not just a bald, unadorned statement of views or opinions on some matter. The candidate is being invited to write a more reflective essay which may well contain any or all of these elements and, at its best, will be both varied and personal.

The difficulties you are likely to encounter in tackling a reflective essay resolve themselves into two main areas: the problem of freeing your thoughts and imagination so that they can range in an interesting way over a mass of possible material and the difficulty of choosing what you are going to include in the essay and organising it into a satisfactory and coherent shape. If, after reading this chapter, you practise with a few of the topics listed on the previous page you will begin to feel your way towards developing a personal pattern for writing reflective essays and you will then be able to apply that pattern to almost any topic. In the meantime, I shall quote some examples in order to indicate what can go into this sort of essay and then briefly discuss some ways of organising your material.

What can be included in a reflective essay?

The simple answer to this question is, 'Almost anything that comes to mind, as long as it may be related either by personal association or by some process of thought with the topic suggested in the question.' Nearly all of these questions lend themselves to stating an opinion in a way which conveys as much your personal tastes as you can. It is not really a matter of justifying your opinion with argument and example in a primarily logical and rational manner. The examiner is not so much inviting you to state a case – for or against serial programmes, or idleness, or travelling by train – as to explore the nature and degree of pleasures you have had from these activities. This exploration of your tastes may be carried on through recounting and commenting on memories and by discriminating between different types of experience.

A personal tone

Your reflective essay is likely to be good if it is an intensely personal piece of writing. You are being invited to write at length about what gives you pleasure and you must do so in a full-blooded and personal manner. Indulge yourself in thinking about and recreating in writing your tastes and enjoyment and then something of your natural pleasure in being alive, in being a thinking, feeling human being with a rich variety of individual experience will convey itself to the reader. This is similar to talking with someone about something that excited you both; as you share experiences, you catch each other's enthusiasm. So, when you are writing about something that excites you, be confident in tone: you are an authority in these matters, the one who desires to share his experience with his reader. It is helpful, also, to assume that your reader is receptive and encouraging, someone who will be as fascinated as you are yourself with the discriminations and judgements that you make about your own experience.

Here, as an example of a strong and unashamed personal tone, are the first few paragraphs from an essay called 'On going a journey' by one of the great English essayists, William Hazlitt (1778–1830).

One of the pleasantest things in the world is going a journey; but I like to go by myself. I can enjoy society in a room; but out of doors, nature is company enough for me . . .

5 I cannot see the wit of walking and talking at the same time. When I am in the country I wish to vegetate like the country. I am not for criticising hedgerows and black cattle. I go out of town in order to forget the town and all that is in it. There are those who for this purpose go to watering-places, and carry
10 the metropolis with them. I like more elbow-room and fewer encumbrances, I like solitude, when I give myself up to it, for the sake of solitude; nor do I ask for

'a friend in my retreat,
Whom I may whisper solitude is sweet.'
15

The soul of a journey is liberty, perfect liberty, to think, feel, do just as one pleases. We go a journey chiefly to be free of all impediments and of all inconveniences; to leave ourselves behind, much more to get rid of others. It is because I want a
20 little breathing-space to muse on indifferent matters . . . that I absent myself from the town for a while, without feeling at a loss the moment I am left by myself. Instead of a friend in a post-chaise or in a Tilbury, to exchange good things with, and vary the same stale topics over again, for once let me have a
25 truce with impertinence. Give me the clear blue sky over my head, and the green turf beneath my feet, a winding road before me, and a three hours' march to dinner – and then to thinking! It is hard if I cannot start some game on these lone heaths. I laugh, I run, I leap, I sing for joy. From the point of
30 yonder rolling cloud I plunge into my past being, and revel there, as the sun-burnt Indian plunges headlong into the wave that wafts him to his native shore. Then long-forgotten things, like 'sunken wrack and sunless treasuries,' burst upon

my eager sight, and I begin to feel, think, and be myself again.

You cannot but notice the confident way in which Hazlitt defines quite precisely what he enjoys and elaborates his opinion by comparing it with other opinions and possible enjoyments. Each sentence rounds out a little more our sense of the pleasure he gets from going on a journey alone. Each sentence adds definition to the quality of his experience. He could not present his position, his taste in journeys more clearly; it is there in the first sentence, 'I like to go by myself.' He gives us a glimpse of what walking in the country with others could be like – 'criticising hedgerows and black cattle' – and reminds us of people who say they want to escape from the town but go to places where all the amenities of town are around them. So he defines his own taste by contrast. Then he begins to say why it is that he so much likes solitude on a journey: it is 'liberty, to think, feel, do just as one pleases' and, after another glance at an alternative way of enjoying oneself in discussion with a friend, he begins to give us a taste of exactly what experience it is that he cherishes when being alone in the countryside. With a few deft strokes he sketches himself on some 'lone heath', plunging into the state of being that is his refreshment. He starts remembering freely and anything can spark off this exploration of himself and his past: 'from the point of yonder rolling cloud I plunge into my past being, and revel there.' All the richness of his life is about him, suddenly discovered like some sunken treasure-ship.

You may not find Hazlitt's style of writing familiar or easy to respond to – the essay was, after all, written some 150 years ago – but you should be able to appreciate the way in which he gradually leads us into a closer awareness of exactly why he prefers to be alone on a journey. There is, furthermore, an uplifting quality about his writing: it conveys a sense of discriminating and whole-hearted enjoyment, which is much to be desired in our world of mediocre pleasures and grey, half-hearted indulgences. Be committed to what you are writing about in an essay on your own tastes. Decide what you like and what you dislike and say so clearly and don't be afraid of defining at length what it is in the experience that particularly satisfies you. The more personal and individual your taste and the more closely you are able to define it, the less likely you will be to bore your reader. You could do worse than take Hazlitt as a model.

Inviting the reader to share your taste

I said earlier that almost anything can be included in an essay in which you are reflecting on your own tastes and interests. The extract from Hazlitt has shown the importance of a personal, convinced tone and the possibility of developing an essay through a sequence of closer definitions of what you are writing about and comparisons with other experiences. I want now to suggest another possibility: that of including sections in your essays which describe very fully some moment, some high-point connected with the taste or interest about which you are writing.

In the extract from Hazlitt, there are no specific scenes or particular memories. Mention of 'the clear blue sky', 'the green turf' and 'a winding road' suggests a scene but does not convey one in particular. It acts rather as a catalyst to ideal fantasies of being in the countryside, fantasies that the reader can easily create for himself out of his own memories. The following passage works, however, in a quite different way, by inviting the reader to share with the author in one very distinctive experience. It is from *The Hunting Sketches* by Ivan Turgenev.

> In the evening Ermolai the hunter and I set out for a 'night stand' . . . It's quite possible, however, that not all my readers know what a night stand is. Therefore hearken, gentlemen.
>
> 5 A quarter of an hour before the setting of the sun, in the spring, you enter a grove with a gun but without a dog. You seek out a spot for yourself somewhere near the edge of the woods, look about you, examine the percussion cap of your gun, and exchange winks with your companion. The quarter
> 10 of an hour has passed. The sun has set, but it's still light in the forest, the air is pure and clear, the birds are chattering away at a great rate, the young grass gleams with the joyous gleam of an emerald. You wait. The inner recesses of the forest grow darker by degrees; the ruby light of the evening glow glides
> 15 slowly over the roots and trunks of the trees, rises higher, passes from the lower branches, as yet almost bare, to the motionless treetops that are now falling into slumber. See, the treetops themselves have grown dim; the rosy-cheeked sky is turning to indigo. The forest smell becomes stronger; there is
> 20 a slight breath of warm dampness; the wind that had burst in so near to you dies away. The birds are falling asleep – not all

of them at the same time, but each according to his kind:
there, the chaffinches have fallen quiet; a few moments later
the hedge sparrows do so; the siskins follow suit. It is
25 growing darker in the forest, ever darker. The trees blend into
great darkling masses; the first tiny stars emerge timorously
in the indigo sky. All the birds are asleep. Only the redstarts
and certain tiny woodpeckers keep whistling from time to
time, drowsily. Finally they, too, have fallen quiet. One more
30 time the sonorous voice of the peewit rang out overhead; a
yellow thrush sadly sounded its call somewhere; a night-
ingale sent out its first choppy note.

Your heart is languishing in expectancy, and suddenly – but it
35 is only hunters who will understand me – suddenly in the
deep quiet there resounds a peculiar sort of cawing and
hissing, you hear the measured upsweep of agile wings, and a
woodcock, its long nose gracefully tilted downward, flies
smoothly out from behind a dark birch to encounter your
40 shot.

There, that's what a 'night stand' means.

I have included this passage from *The Hunting Sketches* in order
to suggest a way in which you might develop an essay, or part of an
essay, which aims to convey to your reader the particular
excitement or pleasure that you derive from the subject you are
writing about. The style of both this extract and the Hazlitt passage
is distinctive and appropriate to the author but an attempt to
imitate either of these styles would probably be disastrous. I have
quoted them so that you may be aware of some possibilities for
developing your essays, of the sort of content that might be
included, rather than that you should attempt to copy a
phraseology and tone which is not likely to attune itself easily with
your own style.

Having said that, let us consider what may be learnt from this
passage. In strong contrast to 'On going a journey', there is no
attempt here to define the pleasure of a 'night stand'. Turgenev
does not compare it with other hunting situations and so, by a
process of discrimination, arrive at a closer statement of what
quality this particular experience holds for him, the quality that
makes it different from any other similar situation. Instead, having
told us his subject, he moves straight into a detailed description of

the circumstances and surroundings. He sets the scene with much knowledgeable reference to the wild life and especially to bird songs and he keeps us waiting for the high-point, the moment of exhilaration. He initiates his reader into an imaginative reconstruction of the moments leading up to the sudden flight of the woodcock, which comes as the culmination of patient waiting and listening. In a word, Turgenev conveys his pleasure not through definition but through description.

Turgenev uses certain techniques of writing which ensure that we respond to this passage as an invitation to become absorbed in the experience of a night stand. These techniques include his direct address to the reader and his shifting of the description into the present tense. We subtly enter this imaginary present. The first descriptive sentence does not specify the present (at a certain time of day, 'in the spring, you enter a grove') but with the statement, 'The quarter of an hour has now passed,' we are there, waiting with Turgenev in the forest. He directs our eyes and our ears, reminds us of the forest smell, of a 'slight breath of warm dampness' and so gradually builds up in us a detailed sense of the atmosphere and reality of the place. The tension mounts and we wonder how the climax of all this waiting, watching and listening will come. When it does come, the author inserts a most effective, short statement: 'but it is only hunters who will understand me.' This momentarily halts the climax and adds to the tension and expectation and it also asserts the exclusive quality of what he is describing, reminding those of us who are not hunters that the author is in possession of a memory and an experience that we have not had. We have the sense of being initiated into something special, something outside of our own lives and, therefore, of being enriched.

I have probably said enough to indicate that a piece of richly-descriptive writing, enabling your reader to appreciate some high point of pleasure connected with your chosen topic, may very effectively be introduced into your essay. The whole essay need not be this sort of densely described material. You could well begin with a paragraph or two of the more general (but still personal) approach we encountered in Hazlitt's essay. If you are writing about your unusual pastime — whether it be hot-air-balloon racing or raising asparagus — you could say firmly what particular pleasures it offers you and why it is more satisfactory than other pastimes. In doing this, you would be conveying something of your own personality and tastes. You might then proceed to describe a characteristic moment of pleasure in more detail.

As an exercise in more richly descriptive reflective writing, I suggest you do the following:

1. Decide on a topic, perhaps from the list at the beginning of this chapter. Let it be something of which you have knowledge or experience or, at least, something on which you would like to exercise your imagination.

2. Examine your feelings about the topic and fix on one moment that would contain these feelings in their most intense form. If the subject is 'going fishing', what is the most perfect situation you could imagine for fishing, one which will yield the most satisfaction? In contrast, if you have chosen to answer question 5, and are concentrating on the frustrations of car travel, what would be the most heart-sickening moment in the most tedious car-journey you could imagine? You might choose a real memory or an imaginary situation or – what is more usually the case – combine memory and imagination.

3. Decide how you will introduce the experience to the reader and invite him to share it with you. It may be by direct address – 'You leave home having prepared your bait and collected together your tackle. It is still early and ...' – or by more general impersonal statement – 'Most drivers have suffered the agony of being stuck in a traffic jam in the sweltering holiday period when ...' or by simple, narrative reminiscence – 'On one glorious day I climbed from ...'

4. Decide how you will create tension, what descriptive details will defer the climax, how you will create a sense of expectation in your reader so that the moment of most intense feeling comes as something of a revelation. Many of the points about describing places and narrating events made in chapters 5 and 7 are relevant here; if you have difficulty in elaborating the scene, re-read those chapters.

5. Write and enjoy it.

Including information

I have, so far in this chapter, been emphasising that reflective essays should be personal. To be definitely and vigorously present in the essay conveying your thoughts on the subject with precision, or acting as a guide to the reader, as Turgenev does, is the most sure and certain way of making the essay absorbing. There are times, however, when you may wish to write not so much about your experience of the subject as about the subject itself, to give the reader information and insight about matters of which you have some knowledge.

I think that most candidates would be well advised not to devote an entire essay to expounding a subject. It is rarely successful unless the material is presented in a very ordered fashion and the writer knows enough to include a mass of interesting details that will fascinate the reader. It is perhaps better for you to include information incidentally in the essay. For example, if you are writing on 'going fishing', it would be appropriate to include a short paragraph on the bait required for different kinds of fish, or on whatever aspect of the subject you are knowledgeable but it would be unnecessarily limiting to confine yourself to giving technical advice and information on fishing when the subject could be developed in a personal and imaginative way. I am, of course, talking here of general essay topics, not those shorter questions specifically requiring the candidate to impart clear information. Of the latter sort of question, I shall have something to say in the next chapter.

What I want to demonstrate is that, given a little skill, it is quite possible for information or explanation to be given in the context of an essay primarily concerned with the writer's feelings about and experience of some subject of personal interest. The presence of detailed information may then add an effective new facet to an essay which will appeal to the reader on a number of different levels.

The following passage will demonstrate what can be done in the way of including a variety of material within a single structured framework, the framework being, in this case, a long walking holiday. It is from *Journey through Britain* by John Hillaby.

Across the marsh, not far from Bridgwater as the heron flies, is the Isle of Avalon. At nearby Cadbury archaeologists had found remains of a Celtic chief who might, they thought, have

been King Arthur. Was Cadbury Camelot? The only evidence
that the perfect king and his adulterous wife had lived there –
assuming they were both flesh-and-blood people – is pretty
thin. It rests on a statement by John Leland, the sixteenth-
century antiquarian, who said the place was known to local
folk as Camelot "and they have heard sat that King Arthur
much resorted there". Modern historians can add substan-
tially nothing to this fragment of gossip, but for all that I
decided to have a look at the place.

This is far from easy. Beyond the town bridge you strike the
marsh that lies between the Quantocks and the more
northerly Mendips. This is what locals call the Moors and
geologists the great plain of Somerset. Avalon and the other
mounds in the marsh used to be islands in a shallow sea. In
contrast to the rolling downs of the day before, the landscape
seemed to be curiously Dutch-like and two-dimensional, a
waste-land criss-crossed with canals and willow-fringed
roads.

On the town dump, opposite British Cellophane, some
hundreds of gulls fought hard for foul things periodically
tipped by municipal garbage trucks. The wailing noise
sounded wonderful. Of all birds the herring gull has a
melodious voice and a richer vocabulary than most. It mews
and whines. It trumpets *keeeee-ow, kee-ow, kee-ow* and
when alarmed it laughs nervously *hahahaha.*

Through glasses I looked at one of the creatures in close-up.
Very smooth: white front, grey mantle, yellow beak, and the
cold eyes of a successful general or a cruel blonde.

At the noise of an engine whistle the whole flock rose as one
bird. Up they went, whirling like snowflakes. And, taking
advantage of an airy uplift, they drifted away, slowly, towards
the Isle of Avalon. And on the mere the wailing died away.

I followed them without success. The marsh is almost
impassable and the raised embankment arranged in in-
convenient squares. After chasing up and down the polders
for hours I became painfully aware of my feet and calf
muscles. They were beginning to seize up. I felt the only
chance I had of reaching Bristol the next day was to head
straight – or as straight as you can go in these marshes – for

Cheddar Gorge. Through field-glasses from the highest point
I could find, a deserted windmill, I looked at far-away Avalon.
50   It looked as misty and as insubstantial as the legend.

There is a considerable amount of assorted information here —
history, natural history, physical geography, folklore; Hillaby does
not hesitate to break away from the bald account of his journey to
give us explanation of the mounds in the great plain of Somerset or
to describe in detail the cry and appearance of the herring-gull.
What gives the whole book coherence is the simple progress of his
journey and the fact that he is present all the time, with his thirst
for information, his eye for the unusual, his capacity for enabling us
to see and appreciate whatever caught his attention. He is present
even with his aching feet and calf muscles.

We are back again to the point of recognising the importance of the
personal presence of the author. It is Hillaby's interest in King
Arthur, *his* observation that the Moors seemed 'Dutch-like and
two-dimensional', *his* vision of Avalon as 'misty and insubstantial'
that binds all these elements together. His awareness of himself,
and of a vigorous range of varied interests and responses, sharpens
our interest and whets our appetite for responding to the richness
of life around us.

In your own writing, it is not important to hunt out remarkable or
unusual details to fill up your essays. You will get nowhere if you
strain after such material at the expense of an honest presentation
of what you have noticed and are really interested in. So, be
yourself in your writing but be fully yourself, at your most alert,
enquiring into and observing the detail of what is around you.

As an exercise to conclude this chapter, I suggest that you try the
third topic listed on page 151: 'We would all be idle if we could.'
You can obviously approach it any way you like but, if an approach
does not spring to mind, try this:

1. In the first paragraph examine the quality of the experience that
    is called idleness. Consider the ways in which it appeals or does
    not appeal to you. Make some clear statements about your own
    taste in idleness. (Some of the points made in connection with
    the Hazlitt passage should be relevant here.)

2. Idleness frees us from the blinkered routine of life and enables

us to come alive to all sorts of experience that, in the normal course of events, we cannot afford to bother with. Recollect a day or two spent in this happy condition. What became interesting? What did you spend your time doing? What did you observe and how did you feel? Put yourself in a definite place and make sure that the sense of your presence responding to a whole range of matters is conveyed to the reader.

Chapter 9
Summarising Information and Writing Reports

Most English Language papers contain questions which require the candidate to summarise material which is contained in a long passage. It is usually part of a comprehension exercise though very occasionally, you may be asked to summarise information that you must glean from a set of statistics or present the results of a series of figures in written form. Essentially these questions are designed to test your capacity for thinking clearly and relevantly. You may have to grasp the central argument or sequence of thought in a passage and present it coherently or you may have to collect together information in a passage relating to only one aspect of the subject that is being considered. In a recent paper, for example, candidates were required to read an extract from a richly descriptive guide-book, which contains a full account of the author's feelings about the places he describes, and were then asked to summarise the facts about one particular town. This meant that they had to distinguish between material in the extract which evoked feelings and created atmosphere and material which simply conveyed information.

The art of summarising information or of picking out what is relevant to one topic from a whole mass of material is one that we use constantly. Whenever we tell a friend about a book we have read, or a film we have seen, we summarise its plot, reducing it to essentials. Every time we read a book or newspaper, we pick out what seems relevant to our own thoughts on the subject and very often ignore much of its contents. So, although in the context of an examination, this may seem an artificial exercise, it is a very important skill which must be carefully developed. It is doing in a formal way what your mind does all the time.

Few examination boards set the most straightforward type of summary question, which is the précis, in which the candidate is given a set passage and asked to reduce it to its basic elements, using his own words. Since, however, the précis is a very good way of isolating the basic thought-processes involved in any type of summarising, I shall start by suggesting that you do write a précis before proceeding to the second exercise in this chapter, which will ask you to search through a passage collecting only the information relevant to one particular topic. Finally, I shall have something to say briefly about writing reports.

Writing a précis

1. Nothing can be achieved without a thorough and careful reading of the set passage. You should examine it closely several times, making sure that you fully understand its theme and its main ideas.

2. Jot down the main points in the form of notes. To begin with you would keep these points in their original order, although later you may find it useful to rearrange them.

3. Make a rough version of your summary, using all the main points from your notes but joining them into complete sentences and using your own words. Do not lift whole phrases or sentences from the original passage.

4. Having completed your rough copy, you should look through it carefully with two things in mind: first of all, that it is the correct length required by the examiner — if it contains fewer words than are specified by the examiner, then you have not included all the main points; if it contains more words, then you have included irrelevant material — and, secondly, you should make sure that it is a piece of good English prose. Try to ensure that all clumsy expression is corrected and that the sentences flow smoothly.

5. Having checked the improved rough copy against the set passage to make sure that you have included the main points and only the main points and that you have not borrowed too many words or phrases from the original, write out a neat and accurate final copy.

Some common faults
1. Avoid using elaborate language or figurative language. Your task is to write simple, clear, precise prose and not to reproduce any of the stylistic effects of the original passage. Similarly, avoid any vagueness in your language: this will be the result of not having thought carefully enough about the material in the passage.

2. Be sure that you maintain the balance of material expressed in the original passage. Each idea in your summary should maintain the same degree of prominence and importance as it had before.

3. In chapter 4, we discussed the ways in which arguments and explanations may be structured and it was shown that an author may often make a particular point and then illustrate it with examples. If you have not thought clearly about the passage as a whole, standing back and seeing its main points, then you will be likely to include material from the passage which is not strictly that of the main argument.

4. A similar danger is the inclusion of your own opinions. When you are writing a summary, you must remember that you are in the position of an unbiased reporter and, at all costs, you must avoid bringing your own opinions or feelings into your summary. An associated fault is the tendency to introduce material which does not appear in the set passage. However much such material might help the argument, it must not be used.

Bearing these points in mind and following the procedure set out above, write a summary of the passage below. You should use between 140 and 160 of your own words. A suggested answer, in the form of rough notes followed by a final copy, may be found on page 218 but do not consult it until you have completed the whole exercise. The passage is from *Jobs and Careers* by Tony Gibson.

There is one snag in this job which very soon presents itself. A school-teacher has a certain right to be heeded, and his class knows it. A youth leader has no rights whatever. Nor has he a "captive audience". He is a friendly intruder upon young people's spare time. He may be brimming over with constructive ideas and stimulating advice, but his time will be wasted if he once forgets that he is making suggestions which no one is obliged to accept.

When the "youth movement" first took shape towards the end of the last century, no one needed to worry about offering his help in the wrong way. The men and women who started organisations like the Boy Scouts and the Boys' Brigade, lads' clubs and girls' clubs, were entering a field where young people were underprivileged and deprived. The leaders were benefactors, and, like the soup-kitchens which other charitable people established, there was no need to worry about the demand for the goods supplied. Young people in the slums of the East End of Liverpool, in the Tiger Bay of the Cardiff Docks, in the Gorbals, were starving for warmth, light, clean surroundings and the companionship of dedicated Christian workers who made them feel they mattered, and who brought discipline and order which gave them self-respect.

The pioneers did a first-class job for the young people of their own day, and we owe them a lot. But times have changed: the needs of young people have changed, and so the job of the youth leader must change too. He cannot expect people to queue quietly for what he chooses to dish out. Youth work is now a service, not a charity.

What is a modern youth leader up against?

There are three white elephants that most youth organisations inherit from the past, as you may have noticed yourself. First, make-do premises, frequently schoolrooms or church halls borrowed for the evening – along with the idea that such makeshifts are quite good enough for youth. Second, the mistaken idea that the Programme of Activities is the sole responsibility of an adult leader. This means that instead of being the steward or secretary of the kind of Club to which adults belong, he is just another Headmaster, arranging a curriculum. The third white elephant that burdens modern youth organisations is the well-intentioned but hopelessly negative attitude – that the be-all and end-all of clubs is "to keep youngsters off the streets"

Let us now move on to tackling a type of summary work which, in one form or another, is invariably included in English papers, often as part of a more varied comprehension exercise. This is the question which requires candidates to search through a passage to collect only the information relevant to the topic stated in the question. The process is exactly the same as that applied to writing a précis. From the information given in the following passage (from *Portrait of Elmbury* by John Moore) write a paragraph of no more than 110 words summarising the reasons why the slum-dwellers did not want to move. A suggested answer – rough notes and final copy – may be found on page 219.

All this liveliness, the Festival controversy, "Macbeth", the new factories a-building, the charabancs full of trippers and fishermen, caused Elmbury's queer hotch-potch to boil and bubble merrily all through the summer and autumn. The periodic row about slums and housing blew up again in the Council. Elmbury was making an honest attempt to clean up its appalling alleys and had built a small satellite town, consisting mainly of workmen's cottages, on some parkland two miles away. There were plenty of sites where more houses could be built if necessary, but this didn't entirely solve the problem. In the first place it was often difficult to persuade the slum-dwellers to move; for many of the older people, strange as it may seem, had a sentimental attachment to their own hovel and to their own squalid surroundings. The new housing estate, with its gardens, its trees, its little patches of green, seemed to them a howling wilderness. They said in effect: Our alley may not be very beautiful or very comfortable, but it is all we know, all we have ever known; surely you will not uproot us at our time of life? As far as the old people were concerned, the plea seemed justified. Unfortunately they generally lived with their children, upon whom they were dependent and who in turn had young children; and it was these whom we wanted to save from the slums.

The second difficulty was the cost of the new houses. The rents were higher than many of the Alley-dwellers could afford; and the twopenny bus fare into Elmbury, if they worked there, or if they wanted a drink in the evening, was an additional charge upon their slender means. The teetotallers had seen to it, of course, that there was no pub in the satellite town; and this was another hardship on the old people who, while they lived in Elmbury, had always been able to hobble across to the Wheatsheaf or the George, but who were too infirm to manage the longer walk to the bus-stop and the journey in the crowded bus. The warmth, the cheer, the fellowship of their local pub had meant a great deal to them. Fresh air, clean wallpaper, a bath they didn't use and a garden they couldn't cultivate were no adequate substitutes.

The third problem was, of course, the attitude of the slum-landlords, some of whom sat on the council. The only way of shifting the population of the alleys was to condemn the least habitable dwellings; and the council showed itself extremely reluctant to condemn houses owned by such people as the Deputy Mayor, the oldest Councillor, and the most influential Alderman.

Writing reports

Often the examination paper will ask candidates to write reports on specific subjects or events; an accident or a society meeting, for example, or a matter of general, public concern. In this type of question, your material is usually provided for you on the exam. paper itself, often in note form, and all you have to do is to write it up in good straightforward English. Your approach here should be very similar to your approach to writing up a summary. Get the facts in their most appropriate order and pay special attention to your style, making sure that it is clear and simple. Do not concern yourself with irrelevant information, but concentrate solely on that material which seems to be essential. Also, as in writing summaries, you should normally avoid expressing your personal opinions and you should avoid importing any additional material, unless the question makes it clear that this is acceptable. If you are given no material upon which to base your report, you must, of course, do your best to invent suitable information. This can quite often be done from your own experience, and you should compose your own rough notes before you begin to write the report itself. Some exercises for you to practise these skills follow, but first, a word about simple, clear writing.

Clear, simple English

The phrase has recurred throughout our discussion of writing concerned with presenting information and summarising information and is, indeed, vitally applicable to all comprehension work. Every comprehension question you answer should be dealt with in simple, clear prose without any jargon or language that would normally be used in a specialised setting. To illustrate what I mean and to give you some practice in sensing what constitutes a clear, simple style, here is a short exercise recently set by one of the examining boards. It should prove useful in demonstrating how your own style can be distinctively different from these artificial or specialised styles.

Write out the following in simpler, clearer English:

1. In the event of a breakdown in the negotiations between management and shop floor, industrial action by the latter appears inevitable. (Company report.)

2. In this sub-standard match, Everton clawed their way into a victory position by their aggressive approach, although Ipswich had every chance to pocket the points before half-time. (Football report.)

3. David Cassidy's latest disc, released this week, will have sufficient appeal to the teenyboppers to make it another chart-buster. (Pop report.)

4. He is an extrovert who shines in extra-curricular activities but tends to be a disruptive influence in the classroom situation. (School report.)

Practice exercises in writing reports

1. Write a report showing how a small village, a few miles from your nearest town, can be suitably developed. You should give the village a name, consider the following points and spend about three quarters of an hour on this exercise.
   (a) One factory already being built on the south side of the river – good sites for others.
   (b) Frequent bus and train services to town.
   (c) Disused RAF station – great area available – near factory sites – suitable for housing estate.
   (d) On north side of river, old village – beautiful parkland – buildings dating from fifteenth century – beauty and historic interest – must be preserved. Outlying residential district suggested.
   (e) Main street must be widened – demolish ugly nineteenth-century shops of east side and rebuild – preserve beautiful old houses on opposite side.
   (f) Department of the Environment already planning new bridge across the river in vicinity of village.

2. This exercise requires you to write a report for or against an airport near where you live. It is rather less prescribed than the previous one and invites you to use some or all of the following points and to include any of your own as you write a suitably expanded account.

noise
passenger service
freight service
work in the area
agricultural land lost
effect on historic buildings
links with other cities

3. Finally, here is a rather different exercise concerned with the use of information within well-defined limits. You will need to concentrate not only on the relevance of the information but also on the style or tone appropriate to the writing required. Since it involves the writing of letters, you may care to refer to the following chapter before starting the exercise.

Information about a house, 2 Tiberius Crescent, Sandford, Staffordshire, owned by Mr Robert Garland:

Built 1913 — semi-detached.
Brick with slate roof.
Cellars (rather damp).
Bathroom (in original state).
Three reception rooms.
Small kitchen (un-modernised).
Four bedrooms.

Outside:

Rear garden of approximately half an acre — with dilapidated potting-shed and greenhouse — overgrown and needing attention.
Front garden very small — paved area and entrance to coal cellar.
No garage or garage space.

Situated within half a mile of town centre; quarter of a mile from nearest school. Once a good area — now two factories nearby.

Mr Garland was trying to sell his house, and inserted a very brief advertisement in the *Sandford Times*. Mr James Smith, who lived in Hawley, Lancashire, saw the advertisement and wrote to Mr Garland requesting further details. Mr Garland's reply, though strictly truthful, made the house appear a very desirable property: he was anxious to sell.

Write this letter, as from 2 Tiberius Crescent. You may add to the points given above if you wish but remember that Mr Garland was a clever man who made the house seem much better than it was without actually lying about it.

Chapter 10
Writing Letters and
Stating Opinions

Questions inviting the candidate to write a letter are quite frequently included in the examination and they should not present any major problems to you. Most of the skills that are involved in writing a good personal letter have, in any case, been indicated in previous chapters. For example, in a personal, friendly letter you might want to write about some experiences you have had recently and the sort of letter you would produce is unlikely to be very different from essay subjects that I have suggested in chapters 5 and 7. If it is a first letter to a penfriend, you might want to include an account of your hobbies or personal interests and chapter 8 should be helpful. The only additional point to be made here is that personal letters must be *personal*. Throughout the sections of this book dealing with writing skills, I have emphasised that, if your writing is not to be a boring examination exercise, you must be present in it, conveying your own unique individual view of what is around you; the way you see things, the way you feel about people and experiences must come across to the reader. Nowhere is this more important than in a personal letter. You might think of it as being a substitute for actually being with someone and, if it does not convey your real experience and feelings, then it will be offering very little to your friend. For most people, letters are the only opportunity to be creative and personal in writing, since few of us are writing novels and poetry in our spare time, so it is worth while regarding your letters as a rich opportunity to apply and develop your writing skills.

However, many recent examination questions requiring letter-writing have been designed not so much to test the candidate's capacity to write personally as his capacity to write in a more detached, impersonal manner. The degree of impersonality will, of course, depend on the purpose of the letter and how well the writer knows his correspondent. Some of these questions require the candidate to convey clear instructions or simple description to an acquaintance; others require the statement of opinions or a reply to a provocative point of view. Another type of letter may test the candidate's skill in dealing tactfully with an awkward situation, such as rejecting an invitation without giving offence. In this chapter I shall be concentrating on this rather more detached style of letter-writing but, before moving on to consider the content of and approach to such writing, let us revise briefly the rules for laying out letters.

The intimate letter

This type of letter can be much modified to suit your needs and the degree of intimacy but there is a generally agreed format.

18 Brandy Road,
Sherriton,
Oxfordshire.
24th July, 1975

Dear Dick,

      I feel that I want very much to write and thank you for the . . .

        . . . and I hope we may be able to repeat it soon.

    Love,
      Betty.

Remember to apply the following rules:

1. Your address should appear in the top right-hand corner of the page and its separate parts should appear on separate lines. You should put a comma at the end of each line except the last, where there should be a full-stop. A full-stop should, of course, follow any abbreviations, such as 'Rd.', if used. You should never put your own name above the address.

2. The date appears below the address and should be written as it is in the above letter.

3. On the line below the date and on the left-hand side of the page, you should write the salutation (e.g. 'Dear Dick,'). It is followed by a comma and the letter begins with a capital letter on the line below. Use paragraphs throughout the letter in the normal way.

4. Put the conclusion, in this case 'Love', on the line beneath the letter itself about half-way across the page. It should be

followed by a comma. Your signature should appear on the next line. If you are writing to someone who is an acquaintance rather than a friend, you would be likely to use 'Yours sincerely,' or 'Yours truly,'. Note that 'Yours' begins with a capital letter and does not contain an apostrophe, and that 'sincerely' or 'truly' begins with a small letter.

The semi-formal letter

> 'The Kennels',
> 3 Brandy Avenue,
> Barton.
> 24th July, 1975

Mr D. G. Sebastian,
4 Broadway,
Barton.
Dear Mr Sebastian,

I have been asked to invite you to speak to the Youth Group which meets in St Claire's Church on the subject of . . .

. . . and I would be delighted to give you any further information about the group.

I shall look forward to hearing from you.

> Yours sincerely,
> William Bear.

1. This differs from the intimate letter in that the address of the person to whom you are writing appears, along with his name, above the salutation on the left-hand side of the page.

2. When you know the name of the person to whom you are writing, it is appropriate to conclude the letter with 'Yours sincerely'.

The formal letter
This would be set out in exactly the same way as the semi-formal letter, the only differences being:

1. Instead of the recipient's name (Mr D. G. Sebastian) you would

put his title or position (e.g. The Manager, The Headmistress) above his or her address.

2. The salutation would be 'Dear Sir,' or 'Dear Madam,'.

3. The letter would conclude with 'Yours faithfully,'.

The reader's point of view

After our brief review of the mechanics of letter-writing, let us consider the more difficult aspects of good correspondence, the skills and thought-processes that are involved in creating a letter that will effectively communicate with your reader. Here are some examples of questions that have recently been set in the examination:

1. You have just returned from a month's stay with a foreign pen-friend. He/she is coming to stay with you in a few weeks. Write a letter thanking his/her family for their hospitality and suggesting some arrangements for the return visit.

2. A pen-friend from Africa or India has asked you to describe the house you live in and the district where it is situated. Write a reply.

3. Write a letter to a local farmer or landowner asking for permission for a cross-country race to be run over his land. The date, time, route and your proposed precautions against damage should be some of the points mentioned.

4. Write two letters, each of 150–250 words. The first should make clear to the reader a situation you have experienced or imagined (e.g. a projected outing, a quarrel with a friend, a family problem, an incident at school). The second should be a reply to the first. (You should make clear who is writing each letter.)

The first thing to do before you start writing is to get clear in your own mind the exact circumstances of writing, the sort of person your reader is and the general content of your letter. You need to let your imagination run free and then make some definite decisions. For example, in approaching question 1, you need to decide where your pen-friend lives because that will affect the journey he is going to make and will enable you to make some references to things you did in or near his home. A letter which thanks people for their hospitality but does not make any appreciative comments about what actually happened when you were with them is not likely to convince them that they were very successful in entertaining you. It is necessary to reconstruct or imagine some quite precise details, for example, long, carefully presented meals with a French family or a visit to a particularly memorable place. If you want to say that the family, or, better, one member of the family, was very considerate of your feelings of uncertainty when you first arrived, then decide precisely how that consideration showed itself.

It is equally important to have some idea of the personality of your reader and it may be very effective if you refer to his or her character or attitudes. If you know that your foreign friend is a very sensible person who has travelled before, you might find something like this appropriate:

> I am sure that you will be much less concerned about the journey than I was and will not need detailed instructions from me. However, you might have difficulty at x in finding the platform from which the train goes. You will not have much time, so go . . .

Similarly, in answering question 3, you might say that you know that your reader is keen to encourage the local youth club, or whichever body is organising the cross-country race, and, having allowed this sort of event to take place before on his land, you hope that he will give permission again. Equally well, you might say that the strong stand he took against some vandals who recently broke through one of his fences and allowed his cattle to stray on to the road makes you feel that he would regard your request with some disquiet. At this point, you would naturally reassure him that all your members live in the country and are equally concerned to preserve the countryside code.

The main point that I am making about writing this sort of letter is that you should be constantly aware that it is being written for one particular person who has his own distinctive personality, his own background, which may be very different from yours, and his own values and concerns. On the most superficial level, it would be a nonsense to write to your African friend of question 2 asserting that your house is situated in a typical suburban estate, such as one might find in any town in England. The purpose of that question is to test your capacity for looking afresh at your own environment so that you can convey its characteristics to someone who has no previous experience of a similar place. It all boils down to writing intelligently and considerately to someone and looking at the content of your letter from the receiver's point of view.

Consider how these points would apply in answering the fourth question. Here the candidate is required to write two letters, the second being a reply to the first. If the first letter (from A) describes a quarrel with a friend (B), you would need to decide the writer's motives for wanting to communicate this experience to someone else (C), who might be another friend. It could be that A is seriously concerned to re-establish his damaged relationship and seeks advice on this from C. What is perhaps more likely is that A feels aggrieved or guilty about the quarrel and wants C either to commiserate or to agree that he was right in taking his stand against B. He might want his correspondent to join with him in agreeing that B is 'an impossible person'. There is a considerable range of possible motives behind the urge to write a letter describing a quarrel and the reply is likely to raise at least as many questions in your mind. If C is a sympathetic person and a close friend of A, then he would probably comply with A's implied request for moral support. A neat complexity could, however, be added to the situation by making C a friend of B as well as of A. His letter would then be likely to present a balance of loyalties, supporting A whilst defending B.

What emerges is that you must, in tackling a letter, ask yourself precise questions about the details in the situation on which you are corresponding. You must get clear in your mind why the letter is being written and what the writer is thinking and feeling about his correspondent. Whether you are 'being yourself' or fictional-ising the character of the letter-writer, you must be sure of what sort of response you are anticipating from your correspondent. Think out the background of feelings to the letter and this will help you to bring a creative and convincingly human element into the writing.

Letters and opinions

A letter to a newspaper

A letter which you hope will be published in a newspaper is rather different from one which you might write to an individual. Whereas in the latter you would assume a tone suitable for the individual concerned, the newspaper letter is going to be read by a large number of people and you will be concentrating on presenting your opinions as clearly and pointedly as possible and in terms which will yield the greatest possible measure of support for your ideas from the readership of the paper.

The following letter has appeared in your local newspaper:

Dear Sir,

The behaviour of young people today is disgraceful. If I have to catch the four o'clock bus from town I have to fight boys and girls coming home from school. They never offer me a seat even if I'm carrying heavy shopping bags, and if I ask them to stand up all I get is foul language.

What has happened to the old-fashioned virtues of unselfishness, helpfulness and consideration for others?
Yours faithfully,
A. Holford (Mrs).

Write a reply for publication in the newspaper.

The examination paper containing this question stated that no more than twenty minutes should be spent on this letter and that about twenty-five lines, not counting any addresses or conclusion, should be written. I suggest you write such a letter before considering the points made in the following paragraphs.

How would you describe the aim behind the reply that you have written? Did you intend simply to give vent to angry feelings produced by Mrs Holford's wholesale attack on young people? In that case, your letter is unlikely to be much more subtle than hers. All she is really saying is, 'I hate young people and think that all standards of human behaviour are deteriorating.' It would be very limiting for you to reply in a similar manner deploring the rude and demanding attitudes of the elderly.

A slightly more effective response might be to call into question the accuracy of her comments, stating that on numerous occasions you, as a young person, have given up your bus-seat to someone older and that most of your friends do the same. Your aim here would be to prove her wrong and you could extend this approach somewhat by quoting some circumstantial evidence, such as your time of leaving school, which makes it impossible for most pupils to catch the four o'clock bus from town. Again this is a limited approach which is unlikely to gain very much support from the general readership of the paper.

A more subtle approach, that would present you and other young people in a better light, as tolerant, responsible and realistic, would be perhaps to concede that sometimes such inconsideration does arise for various reasons but that you are perturbed that Mrs Holford has had such unusually bad experiences on buses. The major part of your letter could proceed from this gesture of conciliation into a brief discussion of her final sentence. Why should Mrs. Holford imagine that these all-important virtues of 'unselfishness, helpfulness and consideration for others' are 'old-fashioned' when there are so many examples of young people devoting time and energy to various types of voluntary social service? You could expand this from your own experience or that of others. Basically, the candidate is being invited to defend, in the context of a letter, the values of the young generation and if he writes in an intelligent manner appropriate for inclusion in a local paper, he will gain far more marks than if he produces something that is either too facile or too rude for an editor to print.

Developing your opinions

It is clear that, even in the small scope offered by the question we have just considered, there is room for the development of your own opinions and the brief elaboration of those opinions by reference to specific examples, such as the holiday camp for disabled children at which members of your school helped last summer or the decorating and gardening for old people undertaken by a local youth club etc. If you are the sort of person who holds strong opinions and prefers to write argumentatively rather than to create descriptive or narrative essays, then you will find adequate

179

opportunities in the examination papers for writing in this way. There are, however, two aspects of opinionative writing to which I would like to draw your attention. These are related, first of all, to the overall control of an essay and, secondly, to the convincing development of your opinions.

In considering the question of controlling or structuring an argumentative essay, you should re-read chapter 4, 'Understanding Arguments, Opinions and Explanations'. In that chapter, we noted that a writer may often present his opinions obliquely in order that they might emerge with added impact. He may suggest one way of looking at a problem of reacting to a situation and, rejecting it, proceed to elaborate a different reaction. This enables him to convey both a general, perhaps commonly held, view of the issue and to define his own personal stand. One way of controlling your material is, therefore, to make your own position very clear by opposing it to another way of looking at the problem. In chapter 4, I showed how this method of organising opinions and knowledge could be given additional point and focus by using an imaginary objector, someone who would want to disagree with every point the writer is making. If you use this way of organising your material, you could start your essay with a paragraph presenting the opposition's attitude ('Most people are firmly convinced that . . .' or 'Many people feel that it is a good and proper thing to . . .' or 'It is commonly believed that . . .' etc.) and then briefly elaborate the case for the opposition, concluding the paragraph with your own opinion or perhaps with an indication that you are not happy with the commonly-held view of the matter. In the rest of the essay, you could present the various points that an opponent might make and deal with them one by one, finishing up with a firm statement of your personal opinion.

It should by now be obvious to you that preliminary planning of this sort of essay is all-important. Its structure and paragraphing must be clear and you need to work out, before you start the essay, the various points that you will develop in the course of writing it. The structure I have outlined is by no means the only possibility — you could, for example, approach the subject in a far more detached, uncommitted way, giving equal weight to different opinions on the matter before revealing your own view in the final paragraph — but whatever structure you choose, you must plan the essay before starting it. This is a stage which some candidates may find difficult. In the tension and pressure of the examination, the mind has a tendency to go blank and, having decided to write, say, on 'My views of the colour problem in Britain' you may experience an unpleasant sense that you have absolutely no views on the matter at all. If you are stuck in this manner, start thinking of the opinions that other people would be likely to hold. What would your very conservative great-aunt, your headmaster, your liberal-minded English teacher, your closest friend, a left-wing student say about the question? Choose one or two decided viewpoints and jot down the sort of comments they would make. Your own opinions will soon return to you.

One final point related to the convincing presentation of your opinions: a person's views develop quite naturally out of the interaction between his or her general approach to life (right-wing or left-wing, Christian or humanist, etc.) and his or her own experience. Do not leave your experience out of an opinionative essay. It is not merely appropriate but often very convincing if you relate incidents or refer to particular experiences in showing how you have come to hold the opinions you are advocating. Beware of letting such reminiscences get out of hand and so upset the balance and organisation of the essay but do not hesitate to include them as long as you can show clearly how they are relevant to the point you are making and to the development of your argument.

Examiners are, in fact, aware that opinions, if they are worth anything, must be based on experience. It is no accident that the following questions, all concerning youth culture or the generation gap, have appeared in very recent papers set by various boards. There is a strong chance that you will be invited to tackle an essay on some aspect of youth culture. So, if you intend to write an opinionative essay, I suggest you try one of the following questions.

1. The causes of unrest among young people.

2. Is the present a good time in which to be a sixteen-year-old? What do you think?

3. 'You can't tell the boys from the girls. They all look so scruffy.' 'There's no quality in the clothes. They won't last.'

'Ridiculous! Why don't they wear something sensible?'
Write your views on the clothes young people wear today,
commenting, if you wish, on the above criticisms.

4. 'Most young people today wish to be different but seem all to be
   different in the same way.' Discuss.

5. 'Why can't I just be myself, and not what other people want me
   to be?'

6. Student demonstrations. Would you ever take part in one?

7. What ought parents to be worrying about at the moment? (You
   may care to offer three or four examples of things – which may
   include problems like drugs and violence – that parents
   sometimes seem to miss.)

8. 'It's all that the young can do for the old – to shock them and
   keep them up to date' (G. B. Shaw). In what ways do young
   people do this today? Is it true that this is the only thing they
   can do for the old?

Summary of key points and rules in chapter 10

1. Be sure you know how to lay out intimate, semi-formal and
   official or formal letters.

2. You should make intimate, personal letters as richly descriptive
   as any other writing about your own experience.

3. Before answering a question requiring a letter:
   (a) be sure who is writing it and why he is writing it;
   (b) decide the attitude he has towards his correspondent;
   (c) determine clearly the situation the letter relates to and the
   likely response of the correspondent.

4. When writing the letter, keep in mind the character and
   background of the person to whom it is being written. This will
   affect the content and tone of the letter.

5. A letter to a newspaper should aim at arousing maximum
   support from its general readership, so be reasonable.

6. In writing opinionative essays, bear in mind the different structures you can choose and plan the main points before you begin.

7. Use your own memories and specific examples in essays which present opinions, but always make those examples relevant to the argument.

Chapter 11
The Examination

Tactics and skills

If, over a long period of time, you have been working away at the type of exercise that has been included in previous chapters and have been enjoying developing your capacity for writing in imaginative and intelligent ways, you will by now have acquired a considerable range of communication skills. You will be able to read with ever-increasing perception of all that the author has intended to say and you will be more conscious of what you want to say in your own writing and be able to convey these thoughts and feelings in increasingly precise ways. As you contemplate the examination before you, however, you may well feel unsure of yourself and of your ability to cope.

Most people feel nervous at the thought of a test of their capacities and, in the school subject English Language, where a candidate preparing for the examination cannot fall back on revising a body of facts as a final sprint to the finishing line, nervousness is justified. For this reason, it is particularly important to understand exactly what the examination will demand and to exercise careful tactics in approaching it. Tactics are important for they provide a medium through which you can draw on your resources of skills. An army may be vast and powerful but if all that potential force is not skilfully deployed then it may well be beaten in battle. In fact, many candidates are a good deal more able than they think and possess more skills in communication than they are aware of, for these are skills that are often absorbed unconsciously and it simply requires the right conditions of relaxed working within a secure framework for them to be brought into play. If you know the processes that you are going to follow in the examination and can set about writing your script in a controlled manner, feeling relaxed because you know that is required, then you are likely to draw upon far more of your skills in reading and writing than you would if you were flurried and uncertain about the situation. In this short chapter, I shall try to give you some idea of the various tactics that you may use in approaching the different sorts of questions that are included in all GCE Ordinary-level English Language examinations. But first, a word about accuracy.

Care and accuracy

At this stage, in the examination itself, care and accuracy may well be the most important of all the qualities needed to achieve success. Throughout this book, I have been concentrating on approaches to reading and writing that will yield the greatest degree of understanding and perception of the writings of other people and will enable you to see what of interest and imagination may be included in your own essays. I have not said much about the mechanics of writing – using punctuation accurately, spelling correctly, creating coherent sentences and paragraphing properly – but these things are clearly all-important. They are an essential part of communication and are necessary if we are to know at all accurately what we are saying to each other in writing.

The chapter following this one sets out briefly the main rules for accurate writing but we do not, of course, learn to write correctly by an artificial process of learning rules and then applying them. It is more likely that you will have had to learn the rules in the course of making efforts to convey exactly what you want to in writing. It is when you meet a point of difficulty and feel uncertain about how you have written something that you naturally consult the rules and think for a moment about punctuation or sentence structure or spelling. Sometimes while writing, one experiences the feeling that something is not quite right, that the meaning is not clear or the sentence may be interpreted in different ways. When this happens in the examination, the candidate's response may well be to rush forward, glossing over the point of uncertainty, feeling that he cannot afford to take time exercising careful control over minor details when so much remains to be done in such a short time. This is not only a demoralising way of proceeding, for you must inevitably feel that you are not doing justice to yourself, it is also unproductive – for mere inaccurate bulk will not produce a sympathetic response in the examiner. It is more profitable to cultivate the ability to detach yourself for a moment from the situation and just see how you can clarify what you have written or rewrite it in a different way so as to avoid some uncertainty over possible inaccuracies. Accuracy in writing is like good handwriting or like ordinary politeness in talking: it is most noticed when it is absent and when it is there it helps the flow of communication.

Another point where you will have realised the need for care and accuracy in writing is when a sympathetic reader, who wants to understand what you have written, says 'I cannot quite see what you are saying. The general impression is there but it does not seem properly worked out,' or, in reading the description of a conversation, says, 'It is not clear who is speaking at this point,' or 'This part does not make sense. Too many thoughts merge together. They are not presented in clear, separate sentences,' or 'I cannot read that word. I do not seem to have encountered it before.'

In the examination, part of this process of correction and improvement can be included if you set aside time in which you can read over and digest what you have written. It is no good just letting your eyes skim over the page. You need to come to your own script as if you were a sympathetic outsider reading it for the first time. Does it all make sense? Are the thoughts clearly presented or do they have an uncomfortable tendency to slide into one another? Perhaps you have not used full stops accurately or divided the essay into proper paragraphs. Under the pressure of the examination, it is all too easy for a sense of urgency to drive the candidate along so that he writes rapidly without paying enough care and attention to the details of presentation. So, check your work; exercise your own critical faculties on it, as if you were examining your own script. Five minutes at the end of a comprehension exercise or essay spent in correcting errors and looking for inaccuracies will be time well spent.

The essay

The essay offers you the best opportunity on the paper for demonstrating the range of your language skills. To deal well with it, you need to be able to conceive clearly the content of the essay and the particular effects you want it to have upon the reader. You have to be able to maintain in yourself the sense of its over-all shape whilst dealing with the details that will contribute to the finished piece. The essay offers you considerable freedom and so it is particularly important that you should use the time you spend on it as well as you can and that you should know your own strengths well enough to choose the topic that you will be best able to treat in the examination context.

Time and length

Most boards allow one hour for the essay question, some presenting it as a separate paper, allowing a break before the candidate embarks on the remaining questions. One way of splitting up this hour is to spend about ten minutes organising your material, making a few rough notes so that you can quite swiftly begin to feel what shape the essay will take and how it will develop. It may be helpful in this preliminary planning stage to think of it as a sequence of topics, one for each paragraph. The actual length required varies from board to board but 500 words is sometimes suggested or between two and three sides of foolscap length. So, you might expect to write six or seven paragraphs, each of a reasonable length containing five or six sentences. Having established in your mind the general area you are going to cover in the essay – the people, places, incidents you will describe or the ideas or information that you will treat – it is good to make an attempt to think of it as a whole, as something that, in the course of writing, you will create, something that will be satisfying to you and a pleasure for your reader. Have a readership in mind and let the readership be broader than the examiner. Of course, it is only an exercise, a test in language competence, but the fantasy that you are writing a piece that could be read and enjoyed by a large number of people, perhaps even be published, will certainly help you to put forward your best. Don't think of it as a question of filling out a couple of sides of paper with random sentences. You do have something individual and personal to say – that is true of everyone – so bear in mind a sympathetic audience that is interested in knowing about your thoughts and feelings and past experience.

Having spent ten minutes in preparation and established your attitude to the essay, you should proceed to write it, bearing in mind that you will need at least five minutes at the end to read over the work carefully, to correct any obvious mistakes and perhaps to improve your expression and choice of words. During this stage, when you are actually writing the essay, you may encounter one of two difficulties: you might find that the topic you have chosen has set in motion such a welter of associations and thoughts that it is difficult to choose between them; or you might simply dry up, feeling that you have nothing more to say. There is no need at all to panic if either of these difficulties arise. If you cannot easily decide what to include, it is probably because you have lost a sense of your general intention in writing on this topic. Stop for a moment and remind yourself of what you originally intended and of the effect that you want the piece as a whole to have. In particular, consider how you want it to end. Your choice of material should flow towards the conclusion that you have decided on. It is important to avoid the temptation to write too much, in which case the essay can easily become rambling and stray from the point or away from the material that is central. If you keep a sense of control, you will find that the piece of writing will itself create an order and shape. On the other hand, if you feel a slight panic arising at the thought that you have little more to say but do not seem to have said very much, then make a conscious effort to relax your mind so that more of your own personality can be present and be drawn upon. In moments of such difficulty, there are many questions that you can suggest to yourself to lead you deeper into your subject. Much of chapters 5 to 8 in this book were concerned to suggest ways of getting involved in an essay. If you are writing descriptively about a place or a situation involving people, you have only to make the imaginative effort to ask yourself, 'What details might I have seen, heard, smelt, tasted, touched? What might I have thought about? What might I have felt? And how might all of this have affected my actions? Would other people have reacted in the same way?' If you are writing about someone else's character, you only have to envisage that person in a variety of different circumstances and ask yourself similar questions about him. If you are writing an argumentative essay, you might ask yourself, 'What arguments would be presented by people likely to oppose my viewpoint and how would I meet those arguments?' Do not forget that every piece of writing is, to a greater or lesser degree, an exploration; your essay is unlikely to have much impact if you have discovered nothing whilst writing it nor combined your thoughts or feelings or associations in a fresh way.

One final point related to length and time is an obvious piece of advice. Most of the suggestions for writing that I have included in this book have been open-ended in the sense that I have not indicated the amount of material you should include. For a week or two before the examination, you would do well to practise writing essays within the time-limit set by your particular examination board. You will soon discover, in these rehearsals, where your own difficulties are likely to arise and will gain practice in coping with the problems of too much or too little material.

Choosing your topic

A considerable choice of essay topic is offered by most boards and, in selecting one, you should be guided by a knowledge of your own abilities and preferences. Even if you have merely read through chapters 5 to 10 in this book, you will have realised the range of different types of writing that might be suggested by the essay titles on an examination paper. They could be roughly categorised as: descriptive, narrative, reflective, argumentative or factual. Of course, combinations of these can sometimes be applied to one title, just as one title may frequently be treated in different ways.

It is impossible to guide candidates on how to make the best choice of title for their essay. Only you know what your interests and abilities are, but it is worth pointing out that the most convincing essays are most often those written from personal experience. Unless you have an extremely inventive imagination, you will normally find it easier to write about things which happened to you personally, or about your own ideas on certain topics. Essays which evolve from the writer's own thoughts and experiences tend to be more natural and to commend themselves to any reader. Whether you choose to describe a place or people, to tell a story or to write about your own tastes, likes and dislikes, or to present arguments or information, allow your own experience and personality to permeate the whole essay. Try the different types of essay from the suggestions included in appropriate chapters in this book and get to know the type of writing that most satisfies you and enables you to be yourself. Before you go into the examination room, you should have some idea of the sort of essay you would like to write. That does not mean that you should hope for any specific topic but simply that you should have decided whether you want to write a story or about a character or whatever. This will save time and unnecessary anxiety of choice. If you have understood and practised the processes of writing in at least a couple of the styles we have considered, then you should have no trouble in choosing your topic without delay and in settling down to plan your essay.

The comprehension exercise

The comprehension exercise, in one form or another, comprises most of what remains of the English Language examination, once the essay is complete. Passages set vary considerably, even amongst the papers of the same board. Occasionally a piece of verse may be set but the majority of passages will be in prose, which can be of any type. You may be presented with a piece of narrative, an extract from a novel or short story, with a purely descriptive or autobiographical passage, or it may be an article from a magazine containing a number of factual details, or a piece of dialogue, taken from a play perhaps, or even a diagram or a series of statistical tables. But, whatever type of passage you are given to study, the basic test is the same. It will be designed to find out if you can understand clearly what you have read, so if you read carefully enough and are alert to the intentions of the author, you should cope with it easily enough. Chapters 2, 3 and 4 in this book have been designed to indicate the likely range of comprehension passages and have offered many exercises, so all I shall do at this stage is to briefly summarise the types of questions you may be asked and the method of approach.

Comprehension questions

There are basically three types of question that may be asked, whatever passage is set:

Vocabulary questions are designed to test your knowledge of the words and phrases used by the writer. You will often be asked to give the meaning of a specific word or phrase as it is used in the passage. In answering these questions, you should make sure that your word or phrase can replace the original word without any alteration of meaning. It is no use giving a meaning which could apply in certain circumstances but which cannot possibly apply in the context of this particular passage. It is also important to use the correct part of speech in your answer; it is not adequate to replace a verb with a noun, for instance.

Questions on subject-matter will usually be straightforward and designed to test how clearly you have understood the material contained in the passage. You may be asked to gather some factual information from what you have read, to isolate the main points, if the passage contains an argument, or to abstract and interpret information given you about a character or about the writer himself.

Questions on style will test how far you have appreciated the way in which the passage is written. You could be asked to explain what effect is created by the use of particular words or phrases or how the author uses various techniques to obtain particular effects, such as a sense of expectation, or what mood or tone he achieves. In answering such questions, you need to examine your own responses to the passage and the feelings that it evokes in you. Some sensitivity is required as well as intelligent understanding.

190

Method of approach

1. Read the whole passage more than once until you are satisfied that you have fully understood both its general meaning and the way that the theme of the passage is elaborated in each paragraph. Try to identify the writer's general intention and the effect that a sympathetic reading of the passage has upon you.

2. Read all the questions and consider each one briefly so that you gain a general idea of the range of topics that you will have to write on. Reading through all the questions on the passage will help you to be more aware of what is in the passage and should also help you to avoid using material in one answer which is required for another one.

3. Write your answers. I would suggest that you keep to the order in which the questions are set, since quite often the more difficult questions come last, when the candidate might be expected to have a greater insight into the passage; but if you do find one question particularly difficult, there would be no objection to you leaving it till later, as long as you take care to number the answers correctly. The most vital thing is that your answer should be short and to the point. Make sure that you do not misread the question and that you obey the instructions implicitly. If you are asked to give a meaning, give one simply and clearly; but if you are asked to explain a meaning, make sure that your answer really is an explanation of why the word is used. If you are asked to quote from the passage, just do that and nothing else. You will not benefit from supplying extra material if it is superfluous. Inclusion of any sort of irrelevance, such as putting in your own views when you are asked to say what the author thinks about something, is a sure recipe for disaster. Above all, try to be precise and accurate, making your answers crystal clear. If what you are trying to say feels confused to you, then search for a simpler way of putting it. Incidentally, it is normal practice to answer all questions in the form of complete sentences unless you are definitely directed to do otherwise.

4. Check your answers carefully. As with the essay, careless mistakes can easily occur and you should leave enough time to read over your work.

One final point which applies to the whole paper: do pay attention to your handwriting. Illegible writing will most surely lose you the sympathy of the examiner. If you include any rough work on the script, be sure to put a line clearly through it.

Chapter 12
Key Rules for Accurate Writing

In this chapter I shall simply present the fundamental rules for using punctuation, for spelling, and for structuring sentences and paragraphs. The chapter will conclude with a survey of some of the most common faults that are found on GCE Ordinary-level scripts. There is not room enough to deal with formal grammar but you should at least know of the various parts of speech – verbs, nouns, pronouns, adjectives, adverbs, prepositions and conjunctions – and how they are used in constructing sentences. If you are uncertain about the parts of speech, I suggest that you consult. I. C. Mathew's *Course Companion* for English, also published by Intercontinental Book Productions. Pages 58–65 in that book offer a clear, brief description of how parts of speech function.

Punctuation

It is not likely that you will be thinking at all clearly if you do not use punctuation marks properly. They are essential if you are to adequately organise what you have to say and communicate clearly with your reader. Too many candidates appear to consider punctuation as an optional extra or try to do without it altogether.

The full-stop

A full-stop should always appear at the end of a sentence, unless that sentence happens to be a question or exclamation, in which case, use the appropriate mark. It is surprising how frequently a candidate will ruin his essays through failure to use full-stops properly; sentences run into one another and all sense of clarity and order is lost. Every time you have written a statement that can stand by itself you have completed a sentence. Remember also that a full-stop at the end of a sentence should always be followed by a capital letter at the beginning of the next.

A full-stop should also follow any abbreviation, such as Dr. or B.Sc. or abbreviations used in addresses, e.g. Rd. or St.

The comma

The comma indicates a shorter pause than a full-stop and is generally used to separate words or phrases in a series, for example,

'He walked past shops, houses, restaurants and churches.' Notice that the comma is usually omitted between the last two words of such a list if they are joined by the word 'and'.

The comma is also used to separate a statement which is inserted into the main sentence, for example, 'The Town Hall, standing back from the road and surrounded by trees, faced him as he turned the last corner'.

Another normal use of the comma occurs when some direct speech is introduced into a sentence, for example, 'They gazed speechless for a long time. At last Mary said, "It's beautiful."'

Generally, however, the use of the comma is very largely a matter of commonsense. Whenever you wish to indicate a short pause in the progress of your writing you should use one.

The semi-colon
The semi-colon is a combination of the full-stop and the comma and it indicates a pause slightly shorter than the former but longer than the latter. It is generally used to separate complete statements which could become separate sentences but are closely linked by subject matter, for example, 'We could wait here; we could go on ahead; neither would make much difference.' Quite often it separates clauses which balance or contrast with each other, for example, 'He was calm and dignified; she was wild and unreasonable.' You could often use a full-stop instead of a semi-colon but the latter may make the final effect smoother and show that the statements are to be closely related to each other.

The colon
The colon is frequently used to separate two statements when the second one, without introducing a new topic, illustrates or adds to the force of the first, for example, 'In the end he had no more hope: the failure of all his efforts had completely overwhelmed him.' The colon may similarly indicate a pause before a list of items which illustrates or elaborates the previous statement, as in this example: 'There are a number of tasks before us: to rebuild our lives, create a new society, care for the weak and the old, etc.'

The question mark
It is nothing other than carelessness that could lead you to omit question marks. They follow every straightforward question. If the question happens to be part of a conversation, the question mark

should appear before the closing inverted commas, as in: '"What makes you so late?" asked the Doctor.' It should also be mentioned that you do not use question marks if you are reporting a question and thus using indirect speech. 'The Doctor asked me why I was late,' is a statement and does not require a question mark.

The exclamation mark

Exclamation marks should be used sparingly and only after sentences which are obviously shouted or exclaimed loudly, for example, 'He came into the room and said, "Get out of here!"' Avoid using exclamation marks to imply a forcefulness or humour in your writing. If the force or wit is there it will speak for itself. It is also quite unnecessary to use more than one exclamation mark after a sentence.

The apostrophe

Apostrophes can be used in two different ways:

1. In abbreviations, where an apostrophe should be used to indicate that certain letters have been omitted; for example, 'it's' for 'it is', 'haven't' for 'have not', 'o'clock' for 'of the clock'. It is very common for candidates to fail to include such apostrophes.

2. To indicate possession, where the apostrophe always follows the possessor concerned. If the possessor is singular (as in 'the boy's bike' or 'my mother's knitting') then the apostrophe preceeds the final 's'. If the possessor is plural (as in 'the ladies' hairdresser') the apostrophe is placed after the final 's'.

The hyphen

Its main use is in the formation of compound words, such as 'dining-car', 'mother-in-law', 'sergeant-major', and it is also used to link certain prefixes to other words, such as 'post-war', 're-assess', 'pro-Labour'. Some writers tend to use pairs of hyphens or dashes to isolate a statement which is inserted into a complex main sentence but the practice should, if possible, be avoided. You should similarly avoid using brackets to separate an expression in parenthesis; commas can usually do the job just as effectively.

Inverted commas

The punctuation of direct speech is dealt with in the next section but inverted commas are also used to indicate titles of things, as in, 'The Call of the Wild' or 'The Concise Oxford Dictionary', and whenever you include a quotation of words used by some other writer or words that are being considered as words without regard to their content. You will notice that I have put all the examples of punctuation usage quoted in this chapter in inverted commas.

The punctuation of direct speech

This presents a number of problems although the first step is quite simple. All the words actually spoken aloud plus any relevant punctuation should be placed in inverted commas. Problems may arise, however, in linking the direct speech with the rest of the sentence. The following examples show the various possibilities:

1. When the direct speech follows the indirect speech:
   Fred said, 'Come over here. I want to show you something.'
   Here the change from indirect to direct speech is indicated by the use of the comma after 'said'. The actual speech has two sentences in it and both of them begin with a capital letter.

2. When the indirect speech follows the direct speech:
   'Come over here. I want to show you something,' said Fred.
   Here the change from direct to indirect speech is indicated by a comma after 'something'. However, had the second sentence of Fred's speech been a question or exclamation, that comma would have been replaced by a question mark or exclamation mark.

3. When the indirect speech appears in between two sentences of direct speech:
   'Come over here,' said Fred. 'I want to show you something.'
   Here the change from direct to indirect speech is indicated by a comma after 'here' and the full-stop indicating the end of the complete sentence appears after 'Fred'.

4. When the indirect speech appears in between two parts of the same sentence of direct speech:
   'If you were to come over here,' said Fred, 'you would see something very interesting.'
   The change from direct speech is marked by a comma after 'here' and the change back again by the comma after 'Fred'. Since he is still speaking the same sentence, 'you' does not start with a capital letter.

The only other vital point to remember when you are using direct speech is to start a fresh paragraph every time the speaker changes. The words of the new speaker should begin the new paragraph. When there are only two or three speakers, it is possible to avoid constantly referring to who is speaking since the mere change of paragraph will indicate the change of speaker. Here is an example:

'Oh, John! Where on earth have you been?' asked Mary. John thought for a while and then said,

'I would really prefer not to tell you at present. It is all far too complicated.'

'That's ridiculous. You know that I have been worrying.'

'I'm sorry, dear. I didn't mean to sound abrupt.' He thought for a space, frowning and then said, 'Well, if you really want to know ...'

Spelling.

There is no easy way to improve spelling. A few rules may help, and these are printed below, but there is no substitute for careful attention to spelling in everyday writing and for consulting a dictionary whenever you feel uncertain about a word. I include some lists of common English words with spelling difficulties on the following pages. When you can spell them all correctly, you will be well on the way to using words accurately in your written work. This section concludes with some pairs of words which candidates very frequently confuse; this is not strictly a matter of spelling but rather a matter of misuse.

Some spelling rules

1. **'ie' and 'ei'** The old rule, 'i' before 'e' except after 'c', is worth remembering although there are some exceptions like 'weird', 'seize' and 'sheik'.

2. **'ful' and 'fully'** Many adjectives end with the letters 'ful', as in 'beautiful', 'wonderful' and 'cheerful'. When these are turned into adverbs the ending becomes 'fully' as in 'beautifully'.

3. **'y' and 'ies'** Nouns which, in the singular, end with 'y' following a consonant, always end 'ies' in the plural; for example, 'cherry' becomes 'cherries', 'city' becomes 'cities'. If

the 'y' follows a vowel, however, the plural is formed by simply adding 's', as in 'valleys'.

4. **'y' and 'ily'** Words ending in 'y' normally change the 'y' to 'i' when 'ly' is added, for example, 'merry' becomes 'merrily'.

5. **'ge' and 'ce'** Words ending in 'ge' or 'ce' keep the 'e' when an ending is added to them, for example, 'courage' becomes 'courageous', 'notice' becomes 'noticeable'.

Some word lists

1. absence   business   coolly
   description   existence   immediately
   leisure   necessary   occurrence
   profession   receive   secretary

2. accommodation   condemn   drunkenness
   forty   insistent   likeable
   niece   procedure   preliminary
   transference   success   wilful

3. belief   conscientious   excessive
   holiday   mischief   organiser
   paralyse   persistent   seize
   thorough   umbrella   vicious

4. accessible   category   eligible
   embarrass   grievous   height
   irrelevant   perseverance   predictable
   sergeant   sheriff   yacht

5. achieve   autumn   benefit
   conscience   disappear   except
   instalment   maintenance   picnicking
   prescription   recommend   solemn

6. beautiful   changeable   development
   guard   humour   lovable
   murmur   panicked   pastime
   pursue   restaurant   view

7. author   ceiling   dissatisfied
   existent   incidentally   knowledge
   neighbour   parallel   queue
   rhythm   sincerely   till

8.	across	amount	awkward
	committee	desirable	keenness
	library	noticeable	possession
	receipt	until	weird
9.	address	anxious	argument
	conceit	conscious	disappoint
	handkerchief	irritable	privilege
	similar	truly	vegetable
10.	assistant	arctic	auxiliary
	comparative	courageous	deceit
	despair	independent	irresistible
	professor	repetition	surprise

Words commonly confused

Here is a selection of words which, because they appear similar at first sight, frequently cause confusion. It would be worth your while making the effort to learn them and then to use them as often as you can until you are sure that you know them.

Accept is a verb meaning to take or receive, for example, 'I am delighted to accept this present.'
Except is a preposition meaning omitting or without, for example, 'We all went except Paul, who stayed at home.'

Affect is a verb meaning to influence, as in 'Bad weather will certainly affect the attendance.'
Effect is a noun meaning a result, as in 'The effect of this drug will be to make you feel very drowsy.'
Less commonly, 'effect' can also be used as a verb meaning to achieve, for example, 'He effected an entrance by means of an open window.'

Coarse is an adjective meaning rough or rude, as in 'His coarse behaviour offended the duchess.'
Course is a noun meaning a direction or path, for example, 'If we had followed the course of the river, we would have reached the sea.'

Council is a noun meaning an assembly of people meeting to discuss, for example, 'The council considered the matter for more than an hour.'

Counsel may be a noun meaning advice, as in 'My counsel is that you should go home at once.' It may also be a verb meaning to give advice, as in 'I counsel you to return home.'

Continual is an adjective meaning at regular intervals, as in 'The continual dripping of the tap was most irritating.'
Continuous is an adjective meaning without a break, for example, 'There was a continuous stream of traffic leaving the city.'

Disinterested is an adjective meaning impartial or unbiased, for example, 'The judge gave his disinterested opinion at the trial.'
Uninterested is an adjective meaning having no interest or bored, for example, 'The boys were completely uninterested in the sewing lesson.'

Dual is an adjective meaning composed of two, as in 'The dual carriageway allowed two lines of traffic to move freely.'
Duel is a noun meaning a combat between two people, for example, 'The two men decided to fight a duel to the death.'

Emigrant is a noun meaning one who leaves his own country, for example, 'Many emigrants from England settled in America.'
Immigrant is a noun meaning one who settles in a new country, that is, every 'emigrant' becomes an 'immigrant' when he enters his new country. The phrase, 'the immigrant problem' refers therefore to the problems associated with settling people from abroad within a country and not to the problems associated with people leaving the country.

Envelop is a verb meaning to surround, as in 'The mist began to envelop the entire city.'
Envelope is a noun meaning a wrapper for a letter, as in 'a stamped addressed envelope'.

Faint is a verb meaning to lose consciousness, as in 'A lot of people faint at the sight of blood.' It may also be a noun meaning loss of consciousness or an adjective meaning indistinct or not loud, for example, 'We heard his faint cries for help in the distance.'
Feint is a noun meaning a pretence or a false attack, as in 'The boxer made a feint with his left, then attacked with his right.'

Hoard is a noun meaning a secret store, for example, 'The miser often counted his hoard of treasure.'

Horde is a noun meaning a vast multitude, as in 'A horde of horsemen attacked the camp.'

Human is an adjective meaning having the attributes of mankind, for example, 'Human beings are the only mammals that habitually walk on two legs.'

Humane is an adjective meaning kind or compassionate, for example, 'A humane soldier will not ill-treat his prisoners-of-war.'

Industrial is an adjective meaning having to do with industry and factories, as in 'The industrial estate contained thirty factories.'

Industrious is an adjective meaning diligent, hardworking, for example, 'The industrious pupil studied carefully every night.'

Loose is an adjective meaning not fixed or not tight, as in 'The loose part could be heard rattling within the machine.'

Lose is a verb meaning to mislay or to be defeated, for example, 'I have no intention of losing this particular battle.'

Moral is an adjective meaning virtuous, as in 'The saint led a very moral life.'

Morale is a noun meaning the spirit of a person or a group, for example, 'The morale of the army was low after their defeat.'

Momentary is an adjective meaning lasting only a very short time, as in 'His momentary fit of anger soon passed.'

Momentous is an adjective meaning of great importance, for example, 'He made the momentous decision to attack at dawn.'

Official may be an adjective meaning from the proper authority, as in the phrase 'official documents' or 'official position'. It can also be a noun meaning a person with authority, for example, 'The official allowed us to enter the court.'

Officious is an adjective meaning doing more than is required or interfering, for example, 'She was an extremely officious woman who always meddled in our affairs.'

Practice is a noun meaning a regular action, as in 'football practice', 'piano practice'.

Practise is a verb meaning to perform habitually, for example, 'We had to practise if we were to improve.' These two words are very frequently confused.

Peace is the noun meaning a state of calm and the opposite of turbulence or war.

Piece is a noun meaning a part or a segment, as in, 'a piece of cake'.

Principal is an adjective meaning of first importance, for example, 'His principal task was to save the city.'

Principal can also be a noun meaning the chief person, for example, the 'Principal' of a college or other institution.

Principle is a noun meaning a basic rule, for example, 'The principles of geometry are not easy to grasp.'

Quiet is an adjective meaning without noise.

Quite is an adverb meaning wholly or completely, as in 'I was quite amazed at the beauty of the place.'

Stationary is an adjective meaning not moving, for example, 'The bus must be stationary before anyone can get on.' Remember, perhaps, 'a for 'alt'.

Stationery is a noun meaning writing materials and paper, for example, 'I had to find some stationery before I could write the letter.'

Weather is a noun meaning the conditions in the atmosphere, rain or sun or cloud.

Whether is a conjunction meaning which of two, for example, 'I did not know whether to believe him or not.'

Structuring sentences and paragraphs

The sentence

One of the worst features of essay-writing, especially among weaker candidates, is the failure to compose a correct sentence. Many candidates, when they settle down to write, seem to be unaware of the basic rules of sentence structure and consequently fail to present their ideas and observations with any sort of clarity. It is likely that such candidates have read so little that they have not become accustomed to what a sentence looks like or what it should contain. Consider the following:

'What did I see at the fair? A mass of multi-coloured roundabouts. A dazzle of sideshows. A motley throng of people. A whirl of merry movement.'

Although the words themselves are quite effective, the basic fault is that, apart from the opening question, none of these is a complete sentence. Every sentence that you write must contain at least one finite verb, so that this passage would become correct English if appropriate verbs were added. Consider the following corrected versions:

'What did I see at the fair: a mass of multi-coloured roundabouts, a dazzle of sideshows, a motley throng of people, a whirl of merry movement?'

'What did I see at the fair? A mass of multi-coloured roundabouts turned amid a dazzle of sideshows, while a motley throng of people watched a whirl of merry movement.'

In the first version, only the punctuation has been changed so that the succession of phrases has become part of the main sentence, which is a question. The writer asks if he saw all these things and will presumably answer his question. In the second version, the verbs 'turned' and 'watched' have been added to create a single sentence which answers the initial question. If you are not writing proper sentences, then you are either being extremely lazy over punctuation or you are not forming your thoughts completely enough, not really grasping what it is you want to say.

Another fault may be a lack of variety in length and construction of sentences. A succession of very short statements may, on occasion, be effective but too often it seems jerky and does not help the reader to appreciate the flow of narrative or ideas. On the other hand, it is unwise to allow your sentences to become so long and complicated that you lose yourself in them and confuse your reader. The best way to improve your sentence structure is to look carefully at pieces of writing that you have completed and read them through as if you were a detached but sympathetic person who has not encountered them before. Does the narrative flow easily? Are the sentences varied in construction? Does the construction of the sentences do justice to the thoughts and feelings that appear to lie behind the writing? If the answer to these questions is 'No', then your sentences are probably too short and too repetitive in construction. If, however, it seems that the actual writing is confusing the issues or material that the writer is trying to communicate, then the sentences probably need shortening and simplifying.

The paragraph

If, when you come to write an essay, you have done adequate preliminary planning and have grasped the overall shape of the essay and the various sections into which it most naturally divides, then paragraphing should prove no problem. However, many candidates still lose marks because they indulge in extremes, either writing the entire essay in one huge paragraph without a break or using dozens of tiny paragraphs, many of them containing only one sentence. Both these extremes will almost certainly be penalised in the examination. An essay of examination length would not normally contain more than five or six paragraphs and within each of these there would be at least four or five sentences.

Common faults in writing

Finally, it may be useful to list a number of faults which tend to appear regularly in examination essays. Many of them occur quite easily if you are not concentrating as you write so it would be a useful exercise for you to check over your written work to see if you have made any of the following mistakes.

Agreement between subject and verb

'The main disadvantages of living alone on a desert island without any contact with the outside world, and nothing to do all day is that one becomes very bored.'

In the sentence above the subject is 'disadvantages' (plural) and it therefore requires the plural form of the verb, 'are', not 'is'. It should also be followed by more than one disadvantage being mentioned. Try to check every verb that you use and make sure that it agrees with its subject.

Misrelated participle

'Leaving the harbour, the bridge presented an impressive sight.' As it stands, this sentence suggests that the bridge was leaving the harbour. This fault can be avoided by reconstructing the sentence without the participle 'leaving':
'As we left the harbour, the bridge presented an impressive sight.'
If you wish to use the participle, make sure that there is another word in the sentence to which it can be related:
'Leaving the harbour, we noticed that the bridge presented an impressive sight.'

Double negative

There is sometimes a tendency for writers to repeat the negative

form and thus convey the opposite meaning to that which they intend:
'I didn't do nothing', or 'I didn't see nobody there.'
One negative is all that is required in such statements:
'I didn't do anything', or 'I didn't see anybody there.'

Prepositions wrongly used

Study the following examples and try to remember the correct usage:

'This book is different from that one.'	— NOT 'different to' or 'different than'.
'I was disgusted with him.'	— NOT 'disgusted at'.
'He suffers from bad feet.'	— NOT 'suffers with'.
'He was killed by a car.'	— NOT 'killed with'.
'You play better than he (does).'	— NOT 'better than him'.
'I agree with your proposal.'	— NOT 'agree to'.

Change of tense

It is a common fault for students to begin an essay in the past tense but to slip into the present tense half-way through, or even to jump from one to the other at random. This could even happen within a single sentence, for example, 'He said that he is coming', instead of 'He said that he was coming.' Inconsistency over tenses usually means that the writer has not clearly defined where he is in relation to his material so, if you find yourself uncertain about what tense you should use, ask yourself whether what you are describing happened wholly in the past or whether you are imagining it as happening in the present, and then be consistent.

One and you

'One can always find parking space if you look long enough.' This sentence contains another example of faulty agreement. You must be consistent and keep the same person throughout, so the two possible correct versions of the sentence are:
'One can always find parking space if one looks long enough.'
'You can always find parking space if you look long enough.'

Everybody and everyone

'We wanted everybody to enjoy themselves.'
This is wrong because the words 'everybody' and 'everyone' are both singular, so the words following them must also be singular. The correct version of this sentence would, therefore, be:
'We wanted everybody to enjoy himself (or herself).'

None

'None of these men are clever.'

As in the previous example, this sentence contains a fault of agreement. 'None' means 'not one' and is, therefore, singular, so the following verb must also be singular:

'None of these men is clever.'

Its and it's

This is one of the most common faults, yet the rule concerning it is quite simple. 'Its' (without an apostrophe) means 'of it' or 'belonging to it', as in 'The dog wagged its tail'. 'It's' (with the apostrophe) is an abbreviation for 'it is'. Be very careful not to confuse the two.

Can and may

'Can' means 'is able to' or 'knows how to', while 'may' means 'is allowed to'. So a person 'may' not leave the room because he has been ordered not to, although he 'can' leave the room because he is able to disobey instructions (perhaps) and he knows how to walk.

There and their

This is perhaps the most common of all faults. 'Their' simply means 'of them' or 'belonging to them', as in 'Their house is up for sale.' 'There', on the other hand, refers to a place, as in 'We went there for our holidays.'

To, too and two

'To' is the preposition which you would use in expressions like 'We went to the cinema.'

'Too' is an adverb indicating an excess of something or other, as in 'We had too much to eat last night.'

'Two' is 2.

Where and were

'Where' is used when referring to a place, as in 'That is the house where I was born.'

'Were' is simply part of the verb 'to be', as in 'We were on our way home.'

Suggested Answers

You should bear in mind that all answers to comprehension questions are likely to vary considerably. You will undoubtedly use different from mine and may, on occasion, interpret the passages differently. Use the following answers as a guide to whether or not you have understood the question and answered it directly. Too often candidates produce material that does not directly answer the question that has been asked.

Chapter 2, page 17
1. Life has proved to be full of problems and difficulties for the boys on the island. There are no simple paths for them to follow in any matter and they find it difficult, as a group, to act responsibly. Their clothes have become tattered and uncomfortable and they have none of the cleanliness and comforts of civilisation.
2. Ralph is, at first, simply walking along and trying to think, until he suddenly realises how difficult and complicated life has become for him. This was an unpleasant contrast to the way he had felt when he first arrived on the island. He decides to try to act with full adult responsibility at the coming assembly and attempts to assume a determined, sensible state of mind. He loses this determination when he notices the state of his clothes and realises how uncivilised the boys' way of life has become. He recognises how much he hates the situation.

Chapter 2, page 20
1. Ernest crosses the road carefully and makes sure that his bag of tools is safe by leaving it each night with the man who looks after the public lavatory. He is over-cautious in everything, even ducking his head when there is no danger of hitting it against the beam over the café doorway. He is careful to move backwards through the crowd when carrying his meal.
2. He is at least able to cope with his loneliness by gaining satisfaction from the ordinary activities of drinking, sleeping and eating. He applies the sharp clean action of a craftsman to the way he eats and gains, we may presume, a similar satisfaction from his work.
3. His experiences in the first world war caused Ernest to adopt his isolated life. The horror of it scarred his mind and made him feel

206

he should have died with others in France. Afterwards, as a guilty survivor, he felt he had no right to mix normally with other people.

4. 'Like a littered invasion beach extending between two headlands of tea urns': this describes the debris lying on the counter in the café and compares it to the debris of a war-time invasion beach. It is particularly effective because it suggests that Ernest sees all of his life in terms of his war-time memories. It subtly prepares the reader for the later revelation of the reason for Ernest's isolation.

'Like music flowing here and there in variations of rhythm': this phrase enables us to appreciate how Ernest heard the many noises of the café. They all merged together in a reassuring, soothing distant sound like that of music. No single noise dominated.

'Life moved under him so that he hardly noticed its progress': the phrase effectively summarises the way Ernest experienced the passing of the years, suggesting that the events going on around him made no more impact upon him than something moving beneath the ground or the sea.

'Till only a dull wordless image remained': Ernest did not remember the thoughts that recurred in him after the war. Eventually, the war became a vague visual image in his mind. The phrase points to the fact that he had even withdrawn from his memories.

Chapter 2, page 26

1. The men rushed to carry out Tiurin's instructions partly because of his position of authority and his powerful personality and partly because they were aware that their food ration depended on the amount of work completed by the team.

2. Shukhov decides to retain his trowel and hide it after work is finished. Senka is prepared to continue helping him.

3. The conflict is between his desire to gain the satisfaction of finishing his work and his fear that the team-leader would get into trouble if the tools were returned late. He resolves the conflict by deciding to hide his trowel and to carry on working alone.

4. Tiurin jokes with Shukhov at this point because he admires the latter's presence of mind, his consideration for the team and his pride in his work. He feels that they are good comrades.

5. Tiurin has realised that time is short if the team is not to be late at the gates and is anxious that the work be concluded.

6. The joke is ironic for the men hate the terrible conditions of their lives and work and the way that they are driven to the point of exhaustion. Yet here Shukhov wants to carry on working. He is feeling exhilarated and the work has restored his self-respect.

7. First of all, he casts an admiring glance over his work because he is satisfied with it, in spite of the fact that every second is vitally important. Secondly, he quickly and efficiently hides his trowel because he had enjoyed using it and, if the opportunity presented itself, would want to use it again.

8. He distinguishes between superstitious fears of the darkness and isolation and the real fear of being in danger of physical punishment.

9. He uses this comparison to show that an athlete may run freely for pleasure whilst Senka and Shukhov had to run in great physical discomfort and weariness to avoid a frightening punishment. The contrast heightens our sense of the constricted life these men had to lead.

10. Tiurin is Shukhov's team-leader, and therefore in authority over him, but, because of the work-spirit for which Shukhov is largely responsible, Tiurin praises him and Shukhov is able to treat Tiurin as an equal. There is a great spirit of good-fellowship between them and they co-operate together fully.

11. When Senka is working with Shukhov, the latter knows that he does not have to explain what he needs in order that they should work efficiently together. Senka seemed to understand automatically and so Shukhov respects Senka and feels that he is the wisest man among them. Later on, Senka endangers his own safety by waiting for Shukhov. The latter appreciates his loyalty and knows that he is a good comrade.

12. His concern for his work is shown in the skilled and efficient way he undertakes it. He wants to use up all the mortar and does not waste material. He takes pleasure in looking over the completed wall and, like all good workmen, he carefully looks after his tools.

13. (a) They are both constantly aware that their lives are controlled at almost every point and that the slightest step out of line may bring disaster upon them. They are, therefore, very careful to keep to the rules and their fear of punishment makes them think ahead over every detail. They do not waste energy because they need every ounce of it to preserve their lives. Senka does not even waste words.

(b) Shukhov has not lost his craftsman's enjoyment of work

and his care to utilise every object in some way and Senka has not lost his loyalty to someone with whom he has worked.

Chapter 2, page 33

1. They both want to remain together and are 'loth to part' but Paul feels guilty because he is expected at home whilst Miriam is absorbed in her desire to show him the bush in the wood.

2. Although the bush already meant much to her, it would mean more if Paul saw it with her and shared her feelings for it. She seems to regard him as a sort of priest who will enable the beauty to come into her deepest being.

3. (a) Her intensity of feeling frightened him. He turned away from such powerful intimacy.
   (b) We are told that he felt anxious as they went through the wood. His question, 'Where?', implies an urgency to have the experience quickly finished. He turns away from her deep intimate gaze and wants to leave before her. Lawrence says that he felt imprisoned and anxious before the bush.
   (c) This expresses his sense of freedom and gives him the reassurance of vigorous physical activity.

4. Miriam needs to touch the roses and to worship them. She focuses a great intensity of feeling on to them to make them part of herself. Paul, in contrast, sees the roses as they are, with a life separate from his own. His comparing them with butterflies suggests this separate existence.

5. 'Only he could make it her own, immortal': the statement concisely summarises Miriam's desire that Paul should hallow her experience of the bush (see answer to question 2 above).
   'Splashing the darkness everywhere with great split stars': this phrase compares the effect of cascading roses with falling water and with the random, thick, brilliantly strewn stars in the night sky. A richness is added to the description by these comparisons.
   'His look seemed to travel down into her': this sentence conveys to us Miriam's sensation of being penetrated by Paul's look; it was so intense, her desire that he share the experience of the bush, that she seemed to draw him into herself.
   'A white, virgin scent': Lawrence describes a scent, which cannot be seen, as something 'white'. This suggests the effect it had on Paul. It was something very pure, so pure that, like a virgin, it had never been touched.
   'Like a delicious delirium in his veins': the phrase expresses Paul's sense of freedom. He is almost drunk with the physical sensation of running.

6. (A full answer to this question from me might well confuse you in *your* interpretation of this relationship but it would seem that Miriam is trying to introduce an intensity into the relationship from which Paul is shying away because it threatens his independence and perhaps his relationship with his home.)

Chapter 2, page 34

1. They are sitting together on the rocky ledge of a cliff overlooking the sea.
2. Something is worrying her and she feels that her weariness is boring Philippe. She is too anxious and weary to respond to his effort to cheer her.
3. Philippe wants to bring peace of mind and ease to Vinca, so he talks of things that are associated with beauty and serenity.
4. Both of them feel that the tea party will be an ordeal in which they must conceal the fact that they are lovers but, whereas Philippe feels that they should go through with the ordeal, Vinca is overwhelmed with the thought they must soon be parted and does not want to waste precious time that could be spent alone with Philippe.
5. They see themselves as having to pretend that they have not reached the adult stage of being in love. They will have to go through the motions of being falsely child-like.
6. He thinks of the ordeal of being without Vinca and of the time that must elapse before they can be permanently together. He recognises that the world does not offer them a place for their love.
7. To Vinca it means the only possible resolution of their love. She sees no way of surviving their separation and wants to refuse such compromise as attending the Jallons' tea and tennis party. Philippe realises what she is doing and feels it as a challenge to his manhood, his capacity for grasping hold on life.
8. He must have felt deeply pleased that Vinca was so utterly devoted to their love and have realised that she was abandoning herself entirely to his care. He was united with her and he knew he had the strength to save them.
9. (a) Philippe saw the possibilites of either allowing Vinca to drag him down with her into the sea or of his taking control of the situation and willing that their love should flourish in the real world.
   (b) He acts as he does because of his natural love for life and

because he is able to assume an adult responsibility for their future.

10. Vinca's ideal of love is an absolute one. She cannot conceive of compromise and feels that death together is the only true way of preserving their love. At the same time, it should be noticed that she feels 'rapturous indignation' and that she accepts Philippe's saving action: it seems to imply that she is perhaps aware of over-dramatising things.

11. 'Like those of a prisoner under sentence of death': Vinca's face expresses her sense of being imprisoned in the demands of the adult world which requires her attendance at the tea and tennis party and her parting from Philippe.

    'In the purity of their frenzied love': their love is so intense that any compromising situation, such as the tennis party, where they must hide it, seems to sully and spoil it.

    'But also as an exacting man': Philippe is an adolescent, poised between childhood and manhood. Though he may feel timid at the difficulties that face them, he knows he must think in an adult and responsible manner.

    'With rapturous indignation': Vinca continues to uphold her belief in their love as too pure to be compromised by accepting the limits of the adult world but she is 'rapturous' because, looking at Philippe, she knows that he has made a manly decision and that she loves him.

Chapter 3, page 47

1. The food was exceptional, a hen cooked in soup, the food on other days being fish and potatoes. A tablecloth and cutlery were used only on Sundays.

2. The thought it suggests is that, in this age, we often disguise things by the language we use, making them seem better than they really are.

3. He has introduced the idea that repetitive food is considered inadequate by most people nowadays.

4. He tells of the effect that the girnel of meal had upon him, when he was a small boy. The girnel was packed tightly with meal which gave out a strong smell. It was from the strong smell that he realised how full the girnel was and so grasped a sense of its total size.

5. 'Virtually' here means 'almost'. They were not entirely self-supporting because they bought some things from the shop.

6. The child did not transfer his feelings for the live pig being

butchered to the small cubes of meat into which the pig was cut. They did not seem to be part of the live pig and he felt quite detached when handling them.

7. Old Fred was different from the rest of the islanders in a number of ways. He had a different occupation. He dressed differently, with collar and straw hat and had a refined accent and manners. He also felt superior to the islanders.

8. (a) 'a thin, sensitive little man, terribly proper.'
   (b) As a child, the author may well have regarded Old Fred as a refined and grand person on the island. He would not then have had sufficiently wide experience to know that Fred's manners were 'pernickety' and 'terribly proper' and might have thought him an example of the average way of life on the mainland.

9. (a) The author knew, even then, as a child, that he was pretending.
   (b) 'An undercurrent' suggests that he did not openly admit to being disappointed. He kept this feeling deep within himself.
   (c) He was too young or sickly to be taken to the Lammas market and seems a sad figure standing alone and watching the cheerful party return from something that he could not enjoy.

10. Life was simple, with a good but repetitive diet, varied only on Sundays. The islanders were almost self-sufficient, apart from the few luxuries they bought at the shop, and they utilised all the resources of the island and the sea. The visit to the Lammas market was the high point of the year and, apart from such occasional trips, the islanders must have been isolated from the mainland.

11. The memory of his nightmare suggests that Edwin Muir was a sensitive child who had some irrational fears, though he also remembers feeling pleased with himself for his work salting the pig-meat. He seems to have been rather more sickly and isolated than the rest of the family and remembers one event when he was alone, watching the others return from the Lammas market, and then being disappointed at not being brought the presents he had wanted. His characteristic feelings seem to have included a sadness beneath the surface.

Chapter 3, page 53

1. He remembers this village because it was a typical Spanish village and also because it was the first one he ever stayed in.

2. The phrase describes the flat-roofed shapes of the houses and their pink colour from the setting sun. The comparison with sugar makes the village seem like a sweet, artificial decoration on the landscape.

3. The word suggests the actual movement of the bell. It makes the sensation of hearing the bell seem very physical.

4. It suggests that they were surprised to see him but his appearance pleased them and, perhaps being shy, they were not loud or impolite in their exclamations.

5. He knew that the tasting of the soup was a test of the inn. He wanted to show that he had no doubts about accepting food and accommodation.

6. (a) The dark, Spanish skin of the child and his desperate movement in the water are conveyed in the comparison.
   (b) The phrase suggests that terror is the same experience whether a person is very young or older.
   (c) The father seems to have been simply experimenting, as if he wanted to test the child's capacity for survival. After the ducking, he smothered the baby with kisses.

7. (a) They were served with wine and allowed to eat their meal.
   (b) Nobody greeted them or spoke to them whilst they ate.

8. 'their meal was their own secret business.'

9. He became confused by the wine and felt uncertain about time and place. He felt so relaxed that he appreciated how similar these people were to characters in his own village. In spite of surface differences, he realised that people were the same everywhere. At the same time, he knew that he was a foreigner, that he had only just begun to understand their way of life and he recognised that they were treating him as a child, learning about life.

10. She seemed unperturbed by the arrival of the author and immediately offered the soup. She watched him closely, as if testing his reaction to the taste, and was quite natural and spontaneously vigorous in her movements, spitting in the fire, roaring to the boy, throwing a bucket at the inn-keeper. At the meal, she kept vigorously encouraging the author, seemed pleased with him and wanted him to eat well.

11. We would not have appreciated the author's internal state of mind, full of all the memories of his days in Spain. The word 'roaring' suggests the very strong impact his experiences had had upon him.

12. The days seemed to merge together in his memory. The days were occupied by the most basic routines of eating, drinking

and sleeping. The main characteristic of that time was the violent heat of the Spanish summer.

Chapter 3, page 56

1. He distinguishes between the private family life within the house and the local community life of the neighbourhood.
2. (a) densely populated working-class districts;
   (b) like a picture composed only of dirty-grey colours;
   (c) the confined living-quarters of the factory workers;
   (d) a determined will to stay alive;
   (e) the streets around were either part of the known local area or they shaded off into being part of another, 'foreign' area.
3. (a) The townspeople call it by this title, although it is merely the more prosperous area.
   (b) The 'better end' is more varied in appearance but this area is full of similar streets and houses. It is all squalid and dirty and badly maintained. This area has no parks like the more prosperous residential areas.
   (c) The phrase implies that the description that follows is seen through the eyes of someone who does not live in the area and does not understand the life of the place.
4. The name evokes a sense of desolation, of a barren piece of countryside. (To some it may well evoke the freedom of the countryside in contrast to the town.)
5. The paragraph has described the terrible conditions in which industrial workers live and the final sentence shows how all this has a depriving effect of the children. It relates the general conditions to actual human life.
6. He refers to the bosses' cars in order to point to the contrast between different ways of life. The bosses do not belong to the close-knit working communities of their employees.
7. He elaborates the idea of 'tribal areas' by giving named examples of streets that belong to one area or another and by including personal memories of his own awareness of his local area and how each contained its own gang of youngsters.
8. The list helps us to realise the life of the area more clearly by giving us examples of typical individuals and by showing us how intimately the people knew each other.
9. (a) The outsider would see the place as dirty, mean, badly maintained, noisy and unwholesome, a place in which human life is totally dominated by the demands of industry. The insider, or person living in the area, would feel a comfortable intimacy with the place and the people and would appreciate the warm human life there.

(b) The author has provided this contrast so that we can gain a more rounded, total view of the area and appreciate the quality of the people's lives.

10. It is up to you to use your imagination and own ideas in answering this!

11. (a) The phrase adds the unpleasant association of some ugly, old, decaying mouth to the description of the terraces.
(b) This phrase describes the vegetation in a scornful manner because it is so straggling and filthy.
(c) The phrase conveys a sinister feeling of being closed in. The houses are overshadowed by great factories and other buildings; they are buried in deep cavities.

Chapter 3, page 63

1. He compares it with distances above ground and gives as an example the distance between London Bridge and Oxford Circus.

2. 'These distances bear no relation to distances above ground.'
(You have all but grasped the point if you quote, 'there is hardly anywhere . . . where a man can stand upright,' but the content of the second paragraph is more general than this statement would imply).

3. The passages are so low that it is almost never possible to stand upright and you frequently have to duck or crawl. The floor is uneven and difficult to walk on and there are tracks and moving tubs to avoid. The air is dust-laden and bad to breathe.

4. He uses 'you' in order that we should appreciate the conditions in the mine by going in imagination with the author into a mine.

5. The word implies that the author feels ashamed of his inability to adjust easily to conditions.

6. The author says that, through the actual experience of visiting a mine, one comes to appreciate, all of a sudden, that some people have to endure lives of which most people have no conception. It is like a revelation and is much more than merely knowing this theoretically.

7. I think he introduces this sentence in order to jolt the reader into wondering if he is the sort of person who would not want to be disturbed by these uncomfortable facts about coal-miners' lives.

8. (a) He presents himself as the average man who discovered what coal-mining is like by visiting a mine. He admits to the difficulties he experienced in moving along the mine passages

and, at the end of the extracts, he shows himself in ease and comfort but not easily recognising the way his comfort depends on the labours of men in terrible working conditions.

(b) He conveys this impression of his being the average thoughtless man because the main point of the writing is to provoke the reader into being less selfishly unaware of the miner's job and he does not want to present himself as directly attacking us.

9. (a) The author demonstrates this idea with a number of examples of activities which ultimately depend on the energy derived from coal.

(b) Orwell demonstrates the ordinary man failing to appreciate his dependence on coal by presenting himself in his own home, finding it difficult to connect his use of domestic coal 'with that far-off labour in the mines' and by giving an example of an ordinary activity – driving a car across northern England – in which we would be unlikely to remember that the miners beneath us are providing the means for the car to move forward.

Chapter 4, page 77

1. (a) City dwellers 'live at many densities, not just one'.
(b) The point that emerges is that there is less overcrowding in city homes than in rural homes.
(c) The authors say that people in cities can get away from crowds whereas experimentally caged rats are trapped in their cages. Two examples of escaping from crowding are the man who chooses to drive to work rather than to use the train and the person who takes a walk in the park.

2. They state that people who are likely to behave abnormally are also likely to be impoverished and therefore to live in the cheaper, more densely-populated parts of cities.

3. It is tempting to assume this because statistics show that major crimes increase as cities grow larger.

4. (a) Tokyo and Hong Kong are very densely-populated cities, yet their crime rates are much smaller than those of small American cities. This shows that the amount of crime is not directly related to the density of city population.

(b) It has been proved that the crime rate increases as the over-all population of a city increases but the crime rate does not have the same relationship with increased crowding within a city.

5. (a) Animal ethologists apparently believe that violence takes place in cities because there is little room to go round and people

need to defend their territory against strangers who may invade it.

(b) 'violent crime most often occurs indoors and between inmates.'

6. The authors suggest that these problems arise from the possibility of sub-culture groups, such as criminals, forming more easily in a city where there is a vast number of different sorts of people. They believe, therefore, that urban crime is the result of social structures rather than of simple crowding.

Chapter 4, page 79

1. (a) 'Everyone has a right to choose what risks he takes, however great they may be.'

(b) He presents himself most clearly in this light in the last paragraph where he says that if giving up smoking did not reduce the danger of disease, then it would not be justifiable to paint so graphically the likelihood of developing such diseases.

2. They pretend that they know all about the health dangers of smoking but they have never faced those dangers in personal terms.

3. He wishes to impress on heavy smokers that they are likely to contract lung cancer and he describes two situations where there is a similar chance of death. He therefore argues by using analogies or comparable situations which emphasise the point.

4. They do not take the risk seriously, partly because they would prefer to carry on smoking, and partly because they may not have experienced the death by lung cancer of a member of their family or one of their friends.

5. Smokers pretend that their coughs are merely 'smokers' cough' and will not face the fact that this cough is likely in old age to develop into bronchitis.

6. He comments on this association because it is an argument put forward by smokers to show that smoking is only one cause of respiratory disease. The author is able to suggest that smokers only bring in air pollution because they cannot personally do anything about it. He is also able to demolish the argument by saying that garage mechanics and London traffic policemen are not more prone to lung cancer than any other sections of the community.

Chapter 4, page 86

1. He thinks it is better than the other two plays because it takes place over a shorter time and has more unity and impact.

2. Beatie's quoting of Ronnie's words is a subtle device because it enables his ideas to enter the play without their appearing pompous and unacceptable, as they would in his mouth. The fact that Beatie only half understands what Ronnie has said makes her seem human and evokes the audience's sympathy.

3. Fraser mentions this incident to demonstrate Beatie's natural spontaneity which is greater than her desire to preach.

4. The main cause of friction is that Beatie wants her family to change and become more aware of culture whilst they are very set in their ways and resistant to change.

5. He writes about her in an appreciative manner, including references to her real love for Ronnie and her 'child-like enthusiasm'. He also quotes incidents which show her ordinary straightforward tastes and admires the way she copes with the crisis when she is hurt and discovers her own real thoughts.

6. The announcement by letter that Ronnie is not coming arrives when the whole family has been gathered to receive him.

7. (a) She is experiencing the pain of being let down by someone she loves and the pain of losing face in front of the family. (b) Beatie says that the workers are exploited by 'commercial artists' because they are mentally lazy. She too has been exploited by Ronnie because she has believed everything he has said without question. Had she been mentally alive with him, she would not have been deceived about his reliability.

8. Fraser interprets the climax of the play as a moment when Beatie becomes an artist in her own right, using her own words with natural strength and vigour. Joan Plowright reinforced the climax by introducing a sudden dance of triumph which expressed in action Beatie's discovery of her natural art.

9. He believes the main theme to be the need of uneducated and uncultured people to learn to trust the genuine natural culture and vitality within themselves and not to depend on a culture which is foisted upon them by other people.

10. Fraser here sees 'culture' as including every type of human activity which involves some skill and knowledge. It is not limited to abstract ideas, literature and the fine arts.

Chapter 9, page 165
Rough notes

One snag – youth leader has no rights – an intruder on young people's time – no one obliged to accept his suggestions.

Early days of youth movement – no one need worry about offering help – young people deprived – wanted the assistance of youth workers – made them feel they mattered – brought self-respect. Early pioneers did good job – times changed – needs of young people changed – job must change – can't expect people to queue for his services – it is a service not a charity.

Problems of youth leader inherited from past – (a) make-do premises; (b) programme responsibility of youth leader; (c) idea that youth clubs are just to keep youngsters off streets.

Final copy

An obvious problem of a youth leader is that he has no definite power. Although he is concerned with their leisure activities, youngsters are not obliged to take any notice of his recommendations.

When youth work first began the young people of the country were so poorly catered for that they needed the help of leaders who could give them an aim in life and a sense of responsibility. However, the passage of time has altered the situation and the modern youth leader is now a servant rather than a public benefactor. His job is further complicated by three particular problems which still prevail. First there are the unsuitable buildings in which he has to work; then there is the idea that he alone is responsible for devising the club's programme; and finally he has to overcome the general feeling that youth clubs only exist to prevent children from getting into mischief.   (152 words)

Chapter 9, page 167
Rough notes

Many older people had sentimental attachment to own hovel – new estate like howling wilderness – don't uproot us at our time of life – old people dependent on children, so whole families stay – cost – rents more than they can afford – extra bus fares – no pub in new estate – old people can't manage the walk and bus journey – miss pub – don't appreciate new amenities.

Final copy

The elderly slum-dwellers would not move because they were reluctant to exchange houses in which they had spent all their lives for a new estate which, in their old age, seemed threateningly distant. If the old people wished to stay, then their families, upon whom they were dependent, would also have to stay. The expenses of the new estate were a further drawback, involving higher rents and extra travelling commitments. The final snag was the absence of any public house. These people had always relied on their local as a social centre and refused to lose it, especially in return for various amenities they did not want. (109 words)

Reading List

Here is my personal choice of novels that you may enjoy. Read as much as you can: newspapers, magazines and factual books as well as plenty of good imaginative fiction.

Kingsley Amis: *Lucky Jim*
Isaac Asimov: *Foundation*
James Baldwin: *Go Tell It on the Mountain*
L. Reid Banks: *The L-shaped Room*
Stan Barstow: *A Kind of Loving*
Brendan Behan: *Borstal Boy*
Ray Bradbury: *The Golden Apples of the Sun*
John Braine: *Room at the Top*
Paul Brickhill: *The Dambusters*
Emily Brontë: *Wuthering Heights*
Albert Camus: *The Outsider*
Truman Capote: *In Cold Blood*
Beverly Clearly: *Fifteen*
Colette: *Ripening Seed*
Joseph Conrad: *Lord Jim*
Stephen Crane: *Red Badge of Courage*
Margaret Drabble: *A Summer Bird-Cage*
William Golding: *The Pyramid*
Graham Greene: *The Power and the Glory.*
Ernest Hemingway: *A Farewell to Arms*
Thor Heyerdahl: *The Kon-Tiki Expedition*
Aldous Huxley: *Brave New World*
D. H. Lawrence: *The Virgin and the Gipsy*
Harper Lee: *To Kill a Mockingbird*
Laurie Lee: *Cider with Rosie*
Gavin Maxwell: *Ring of Bright Water*
George Orwell: *1984*
Boris Pasternak: *Doctor Zhivago*
J. D. Salinger: *The Catcher in the Rye*
John Steinbeck: *The Grapes of Wrath*
Josephine Tey: *The Daughter of Time*
L. Thomas: *This Time Next Week*
John Wain: *Strike the Father Dead*
H. G. Wells: *The Time Machine*
John Wyndham: *The Day of the Triffids*

Acknowledgements

Extract from *The Cathedrals of England* by Harry Batsford and Charles Fry reprinted by permission of the publishers, Batsford Limited.

Extract from *The Age of Improvement* by Asa Briggs reprinted by permission of the publishers, Longman.

Extract from *Mister Johnson* by Joyce Cary reprinted by permission of the Estate of Joyce Cary and Curtis Brown Ltd.

Extract from *The Ripening Seed* by Colette, translated by Roger Senhouse, *Hurry On Down* by John Wain and *Death in Venice* by Thomas Mann reprinted by permission of the publishers, Martin Secker & Warburg Limited.

Extract from *The Waterfall* by Margaret Drabble reprinted by permission of the publishers, Weidenfeld and Nicolson.

Extract from 'How far from the madding crowd?' by Claude S. Fischer and Mark Baldassare first appeared in *New Society, the weekly review of the Social Sciences* (London).

Extract from 'How to Stop' by Christopher Wood in *Common Sense About Smoking* (pp 107–9) by C. M. Fletcher *et al* (Penguin Special, 1963) reprinted by permission of the publishers, Penguin Books Ltd. (copyright © Penguin Books and contributors, 1963, 1965).

Extract from *The Modern Writer and his World* by G. S. Fraser reprinted by permission of Curtis Brown Ltd.

Extract from *Jobs and Careers* by Tony Gibson, published by Victor Gollancz Ltd., reprinted by permission of the author.

Extracts from *Lord of the Flies* by William Golding and *A Girl in Winter* by Philip Larkin reprinted by permission of the publishers, Faber and Faber Ltd.

Extract from *My Apprenticeship* (pp 86–7) by Maxim Gorky, translated by Ronald Wilks (copyright © Ronald Wilks 1974) for Penguin Classics, reprinted by permission of the publishers, Penguin Books Ltd.

Extract from *Journey Through Britain* by John Hillaby reprinted by permission of the publishers, Constable & Co. Ltd.

Extract from *The Uses of Literacy* by Richard Hoggart reprinted by permission of the publishers, Chatto and Windus Ltd.

Extract from 'Counterparts' in *Dubliners* by James Joyce, published by Jonathan Cape Ltd., reprinted by permission of the Executors of the James Joyce Estate.

Extracts from *The Rainbow* and *Sons and Lovers* by D. H.

Lawrence and from *The Fox* (in *The Short Novels of D. H. Lawrence*) published by permission of Laurence Pollinger Ltd. and the Estate of the late Mrs Frieda Lawrence.

Extract from *As I Walked Out One Midsummer Morning* by Laurie Lee reprinted by permission of the publishers, André Deutsch Limited.

Extract from *Portrait of Elmbury* by John Moore, published by William Collins Sons & Co. Ltd., reprinted by permission of A. D. Peters & Co. Ltd.

Extract from *An Autobiography* by Edwin Muir reprinted by permission of Mr Gavin Muir and the publishers, The Hogarth Press.

Extract from 'Down the Mine' from *Selected Essays* by George Orwell, published by Martin Secker & Warburg Limited, reprinted by permission of Mrs Sonia Brownell Orwell and the Orwell Estate.

Extract from *Loneliness of the Long Distance Runner* by Alan Sillitoe reprinted by permission of Star Books.

Extract from *One Day in the Life of Ivan Denisovich* by Alexander Solzhenitsyn reprinted by permission of the publishers, Victor Gollancz Ltd.

The poem 'Adlestrop' from *Collected Poems* by Edward Thomas, published by Faber and Faber Ltd., reprinted by permission of Myfanwy Thomas.

Extract from *The Hunting Sketches* by Ivan Turgenev, translated by Bernard Guilbert Guerney (copyright © 1952 by Bernard Guilbert Guerney) reprinted by arrangement with The New American Library, Inc., New York, N.Y.

Chapters 11 and 12 are largely based on sections from the Key Facts *English Course Companion* by I. C. Mathew, B.A., published by Intercontinental Book Productions in conjunction with Seymour Press Ltd.

Other study aids in the  series

KEY FACTS CARDS

Latin
Julius Caesar
New Testament
German
Macbeth
Geography Regional
English Comprehension
English Language
Economics
Elementary Mathematics
Algebra
Modern Mathematics

English History (1815–1914)
English History (1914–1946)
Chemistry
Physics
Biology
Geometry
Geography
French
Arithmetic & Trigonometry
General Science
Additional Mathematics
Technical Drawing

KEY FACTS COURSE COMPANIONS

Economics
Modern Mathematics
Algebra
Geometry
Arithmetic & Trigonometry
Additional Mathematics

Geography
French
Physics
Chemistry
English
Biology

KEY FACTS A-LEVEL BOOKS

Chemistry
Biology

Pure Mathematics
Physics

KEY FACTS O-LEVEL PASSBOOKS

Modern Mathematics
Geography
Biology
Chemistry
Economics

Physics
English History (1815–1939)
French
English

KEY FACTS O-LEVEL MODEL ANSWERS

Modern Mathematics
Geography
Biology
Chemistry

Physics
English History (1815–1939)
French
English

KEY FACTS REFERENCE LIBRARY

O–Level Biology
O–Level Physics
O–Level Chemistry

O–Level Trad. & Mod. Mathematic
O–Level Geography
O–Level English History (1815–191

KEYFACTS A–LEVEL PASSBOOKS

Physics
Biology

Chemistry
Pure Mathematics